D1452829

DATE DUE

Jan 2013		
	▪	

A FINE WILL BE CHARGED FOR EACH
OVERDUE MATERIAL.

Simone de Beauvoir Writing the Self

Philosophy Becomes Autobiography

Jo-Ann Pilardi

Westport, Connecticut
London

The Library of Congress has catalogued the hardcover edition as follows:

Pilardi, Jo-Ann, 1941–
   Simone de Beauvoir writing the self : philosophy becomes
autobiography / Jo-Ann Pilardi.
      p.   cm.—(Contributions in philosophy, ISSN 0084–926X ; no.
60)
   Includes bibliographical references and index.
   ISBN 0–313–30253–7 (alk. paper)
   1. Beauvoir, Simone de, 1908–   . 2. Self (Philosophy)
I. Title. II. Series.
B2430.B344P55   1999
194—dc21   97–44836

British Library Cataloguing in Publication Data is available.

A hardcover edition of *Simone de Beauvoir Writing the Self* is available from Greenwood
Press, an imprint of Greenwood Publishing Group, Inc. (Contributions in Philosophy,
Number 60; ISBN 0–313–30253–7).

Library of Congress Catalog Card Number: 97–44836
ISBN: 0–275–96334–9

First published in 1999

Praeger Publishers, 88 Post Road West, Westport, CT 06881
An imprint of Greenwood Publishing Group, Inc.

Printed in the United States of America

The paper used in this book complies with the
Permanent Paper Standard issued by the National
Information Standards Organization (Z39.48–1984).

10 9 8 7 6 5 4 3 2 1

In memory of my mother, Nicolina Mascia Pilardi (1916–1998), with gratitude for sharing with me her vibrant life.

Contents

Acknowledgments

Thanks are due to Neil Hertz and Jerome Schneewind, who helped me craft this material originally, as a dissertation for The Johns Hopkins University Humanities Center. Their ideas intrigued me; their kindnesses strengthened me; their humor eased the burden. Richard Macksey also deserves thanks for encouraging me to continue saying what I had to say about Beauvoir; to Catherine Macksey, thanks for reinvigorating my love of the French language.

For gracefully helping with the production of the manuscript through its various stages, thanks go to Elisabetta Linton, Leanne Jisonna, and Betty Pessagno, at Greenwood Press, and to Nina Pearlstein and Wendy Samuels. To Stephannie Faison, thanks for your many kindnesses.

To my son, Dorion Fuchs, whose lively mind was (and is) always happy to be engaged, my ongoing thanks. During the writing of this book, life brought its usual ups and downs, but there was an especially difficult event—at the last stages of manuscript preparation—the death of my beloved mother, Nickie Pilardi. For their continued support, special thanks to my family: my father, William Pilardi; my sisters, Regina Pilardi and Sandra Baxter; my brother, Bill; my daughter-in-law, Michelle Lesane Fuchs: my brothers-in-law, Dan Kelley and Don Baxter; and to my dear friend, Rita Mowery.

To my colleagues at Towson University, I send grateful thanks for their conversations, questions, and help, especially to Jacqueline Wilkotz, Sara Coulter, K Edgington, John Murungi, Rose Ann Christian, Fran Rothstein, and Cindy Gissendanner. Thanks to my students and former students for their engagement with the issues I discuss in this book. A special thanks to Iris Young, Clarinda Harriss, John Rose, and Richard Macksey (again), for finding time to review the manuscript.

My final thanks go to my two-year-old granddaughter, Talia Nicole Fuchs—simply for being her very spirited self.

Introduction

This book is a study of the writings Simone de Beauvoir chose to publish during her lifetime as her philosophical and autobiographical works. It is not a study of letters—neither her own posthumously published letters, nor those of Jean-Paul Sartre to her and others, nor those of others to her or Sartre. This should not be taken to mean that I discount the actual authenticity of any of the volumes of letters published from 1980 (the year of Sartre's death) to the present, or that I believe them to be insignificant. But it does mean that I have drawn my own circle of significance for this book, encompassing only the works Beauvoir chose to publish as philosophy and autobiography. Every circle has its own circumference; now the reader knows the circumference of mine.

Simone de Beauvoir said in her autobiography that the problem of the other became her particular philosophical issue. Through a study of her earliest novels, *She Came to Stay* and *The Blood of Others*, as well as her most famous work, *The Second Sex*, readers might conclude this as well, and only this. In *The Second Sex* she created a new paradigm with which to analyze woman's situation: woman as Other.[1] But the problem of the Other in Beauvoirian thought should be understood as complementary to the problem of the self, as one-half of the familiar, undeconstructed dichotomy of self/other. It's in this light that I offer this book, a study of Beauvoir's notion of the self and its use within her autobiographical writings. This is a study of the *other* side of the Other.

Beauvoir derived the self/other problem from two Continental philosophical sources: (1) Hegel's conception of the self, where the other is presented as a negative definition of the self, and (2) Sartre's interpretation of Husserlian phenomenology, which contrasted the self as "for-itself" to the self as ego.[2] This book is derived primarily from that tradition, specifically from existential phenomenology. But because this book is a study of Beauvoir's notion of the self written in English for an English-speaking audience, it takes account of two issues that are not related to Beauvoir's own writing: (1) the difference in the Anglo-American and Continental philosophical discussions of the self, and (2) the differences in the original texts and the English translations of Beauvoir's writings. I will begin with an account of differences in the two traditions that are significant to a study of the self.

THE EXISTENTIAL-PHENOMENOLOGICAL TRADITION OF THE SELF

In the tradition in which Simone de Beauvoir wrote, existentialism or "existential phenomenology" (the latter is a term she uses occasionally), the self is analyzed primarily through a discussion of consciousness and its "by-product," the ego. These concepts are derived from the Husserlian phenomenological school as interpreted by Sartre. In Husserlian phenomenology, one term for the self is "ego" or "pure ego," called by Husserl "the wonder of all wonders."[3] This is defined as "the identical subject pole of several acts," and it will be transformed into the "transcendental ego" after being subjected to the phenomenological reduction.[4] (Husserl's "pure ego" is not to be confused with the traditional psychological notion of the self, for that notion of the self is *not* defined as capable of being subjected to the phenomenological reduction.)[5]

This problem necessitated the distinction of two types of being: "for-itself" and "in-itself" (intentional and nonintentional). It is on the axis of intentionality then, that the existential-phenomenological problem of the self developed by Sartre and used by Beauvoir turns. My contention will be that Beauvoir then went on to develop another notion of the self, what I call "the gendered self."[6] It is also intentionality, understood in an active sense as the transcendence of the for-itself, that Beauvoir later changed by her conclusion in *The Second Sex* that woman was a transcendence, forced to be an immanence by a patriarchal society. As we will see, though this form of oppression could never be totally effective (i.e., woman cannot ever be reduced to mere immanence, to a thing, to the in-itself), the presence of this oppression would still be the central conflict of a woman's life, according to Beauvoir.

Intentionality is best approached through Edmund Husserl's well-known remark that consciousness is always "consciousness of something."[7]

The movement of consciousness toward some thing, toward an object of which it is aware, is the very structure of consciousness and is what Husserl called "intentionality," the ability of consciousness to "in-tend" toward an object that it perceives. Consciousness "has" acts of intention, either of perception or imagination. All else is nonintentional being, or what Sartre called "being-in-itself," the being which things have. By contrast, Sartre used the term "for-itself," taken from Hegel, to indicate consciousness as a being with transcendence, as distinct from the category of in-itself, the being of things, immanent being.[8]

Husserl had thought that a unifying element he called the "transcendental ego" was necessary to connect the acts of and individualize consciousness. Sartre argued in *The Transcendence of the Ego* that such an element would in fact be foreign to the qualities of consciousness: emptiness, nothingness, and spontaneity.[9] Husserl's "transcendental ego" might signify these, but only these, Sartre insisted. Consciousness, without content of its own, is an intentional movement but not a content; it is "for-itself" but not "in-itself." Because it is not a content, and has no substance, consciousness is impersonal, "an impersonal spontaneity"; this is to say, it doesn't emerge from an "I" or a "self," if "self" is taken as a person, an ego-formation. There is no ego inhabiting consciousness (or vice versa: there is nothing called "consciousness" lodged in an ego), and when an ego can be perceived—and Sartre allows that it can—it is surprisingly not the "owner" of consciousness, but its object; one arising out of the movement of consciousness and derived from consciousness, not prior to it. Because this self is an object, it can be known by consciousness. As the "reflected" or "reflexive" self, it can be studied by consciousness or by others, either formally and scientifically (through the field of psychology) or informally. But it is no longer the for-itself, since that is nothingness, no thing, a non-object. Beauvoir herself went to some trouble to explain this in her second volume of autobiography, *La Force de l'âge*, as she summarized Sartre's innovations in *The Transcendence of the Ego*:

Here he described, in a Husserlian perspective but in opposition to certain of the most recent theories of Husserl, the relation of the self (*le moi*) with consciousness; he established a relation between consciousness (*conscience*) and the psyche (*le psychique*) that he would always maintain: whereas consciousness is an immediate and evident presence to self (*soi*), the psyche is an ensemble of objects which are only apprehended by a reflexive operation and which, like the objects of perception, are only given by profiles. . . . My ego (*mon Ego*) is itself a being in the world, just like the ego of the other. Thus Sartre established one of his earliest and most stubbornly-held beliefs: unreflective consciousness has autonomy; the relation to the self (*au moi*) which, according to La Rouchefoucauld and the French psychological tradition, would pervert our most spontaneous movements, appeared only in certain particular circumstances. . . . This theory and only this, he felt, permitted an escape from solipsism—the "psychic," the ego, existing for the other and for me in the same objective manner.[10]

This is the problem of the self with which Beauvoir began, an opposition between consciousness ("self") as for-itself and self as ego.

DIFFERENCES BETWEEN THE ANGLO-AMERICAN AND CONTINENTAL PHILOSOPHICAL TRADITIONS

In the Anglo-American philosophical tradition, the self is most often described within the context of personal identity (i.e., the unity of a person through time); such questions of unity and identity are most often posed in terms of a philosophy of "mind." Most contemporary Anglo-American discussions of the person, revolving around issues of criteria for individuation and reidentification, differ from the Sartrean (existential-phenomenological) discussion of the self in that the former most often take up the discussion in the field of epistemology and the latter in the field of ethics. Questions of epistemology and perception tend to predominate here, around discussions of the self, not questions of action and choice grounded in intentionality, as in Sartrean philosophy—though issues of perception are there, to be sure, just as issues of moral practice are also apparent in contemporary Anglo-American discussions of the person.[11] Sartre's discussion of the self continually fluctuates within a descriptive-prescriptive tension. It is this tension which Beauvoir took up, in both *The Ethics of Ambiguity* and *The Second Sex*. It is, I believe, her focus on this tension which makes *The Second Sex* such a compelling book for its women readers. Further, what was an ontological description of the transcendence of the for-itself in *The Ethics of Ambiguity* was further complicated in *The Second Sex*, for that book provided a description of an oppressive "situation." Such a "situation," to use Beauvoir's own term, and not a "nature," was responsible for any limitations along gender lines that "women in groups" displayed. Existentialist ethics would provide a program to counteract and overcome that oppressive situation.[12]

Anglo-American philosopher Amelie Oksenberg Rorty synthesizes various approaches to the issue of personal identity in the introduction to her anthology, *The Identities of Persons*.[13] Rorty calls the Sartrean concept the "person as the 'I' of reflective consciousness" position—one held also by Descartes, Locke, Hume, and Kant. Her references to Sartre's analysis of consciousness provide helpful instances of translation from one philosophic idiom to the other. She maintains that, in contrast to the claims of some, personal identity cannot be reduced to the problem of "responsible agency"—that is, the issue of persons as intentional agents:

Even if—*per impossible*—we came to think of responsible agency as an illusion, the problem of the identity of the self, the "I" would remain. What are the conditions for the identity of the reflective, conscious subject of experience, a subject that is not identical with any set of its experiences, memories or traits, but is that which *has* all of them, and can choose either to identify with them or to reject them as alien?[14]

In its most recent form, she claims, this tradition of the self as reflective, conscious subject has evolved into Sartre's (and Heidegger's) analysis of consciousness as non-being.[15] Rorty labels Sartre a "strict constructionist of reflective consciousness identity," or a thinker who claims that merely by the act of reflection itself (an act that consciousness performs), a something—which is a "nothing"—is revealed. This is an allusion to such claims as Heidegger's that *dasein* is the being for whom its being can be a "question."[16] According to Rorty, beyond the "question," and because of the question (of its being), a reflective consciousness can become a "self," an "I": "So strict constructionists find themselves forced to postulate a something-perhaps-a-nothing-I-know-not-what . . . or a pure act of reflection that constitutes itself."[17] Bristling at what she claims is a refusal by strict constructionists to use experience, which would include the experience of an empirical self, Rorty dismisses them as "evangelist[s] in philosophic clothing" who require us to take on faith what cannot be proven.[18] But what, after all, is this empirical self to which she refers, and by what signs might we know it?

In "A Literary Postscript: Characters, Persons, Selves, Individuals," Rorty set out, unfortunately with no documentation and some easy generalizations, to diacritically trace the spaces carved out and the functions performed by such terms as "characters," "persons," "selves," and so on, providing a kind of history of ideas and culture. She claims that the term "self" has been reserved for that which is a possessor of rights and powers, as well as properties and qualities. "Self" includes "person," on one hand, a term which indicates legal empowerment and liability and is based on the claim that one has a choice. But "self" also includes "individual," a term indicating the importance of a human being's specific development, often against society, particularly so that one is differentiated from others.[19] Sartre's human being, under Rorty's typology, is an "individual," and thus overconcerned with "the horrors of choice," since it not only needs to act, but to invent principles upon which to act.[20]

But not all Anglo-American philosophers are insistent on acknowledging the importance of such terminological boundaries. In "Responsibility for Self," Charles Taylor asks: "What is the notion of responsibility which is bound up with our conception of a person or self?" and answers: "beyond the *de facto* characterization of the subject by his (sic) goals, desires, and purposes, a person is a subject who can pose the *de jure* question: is this the kind of being I ought to be, or really want to be?"[21] Quoting sources in the Continental tradition, Taylor defines "persons," that is, "subjects," as those "capable of evaluating what they are, and to the extent that they can shape themselves on this evaluation, are responsible for what they are in a way that other subjects of action and desire (the higher animals, for instance) cannot be said to be."[22] Taylor goes on to conclude that it is in a "responsibility for oneself . . . for radical evaluation implicit in the nature of a strong evaluator" that the essence of our notion of a person lies.[23] Taylor's remarks provide a good example of a blurring of distinctions along the "person-subject-self" continuum, creating a synthesis of the two traditions through a hybrid notion of the person as one who can ask questions about her or his own actions. He skirts the question of identity of self and locates his analysis in the realm of activity, a realm that is identifiable to existential phenomenologists as "intentionality," and in so doing, he distances himself from notions of thinghood or substantiality.

DIFFERENCES IN HOW THE FRENCH AND ENGLISH LANGUAGES SPEAK THE SELF

The difference between the French and English languages in regard to the use of reflexive verbs is important here, in particular, the frequent use in French of reflexive constructions to "self-refer" and, in this manner, to obliquely create a "self." Conversely, one might note that English isolates and reifies a "self" by its more frequent use of noun forms. One grammarian, John Brueckner, claims that "the greatest single difference between French and English verbs lies perhaps in the high frequency of the so-called reflexive French verb . . . [the] pronominal verbs."[24] He points out that French uses such verb forms over ten times as frequently as English, thus requiring a reflexive object in many more cases than English, which customarily omits the object. Because French functions in this manner, a "reflexive noun object" often appears; in many such cases, a "self" also appears. An example from Beauvoir's writing will illustrate this. The first usage of "self" in the English translation of *The Ethics of Ambiguity* is the following: "those who have accepted the dualism have established a hierarchy between body and soul which permits of considering as negligible the part of the self which cannot be saved."[25] The French original here uses *soi-même*—self, or one's self. However, the second appearance of the word "self" in the English edition derives from a French reflexive form of the verb *faire* (to make or do), and not from the pronoun *soi-même*.[26] The original sentence contains four reflexives, though the English translation renders two of them directly through the use of "self" or "oneself": "It has been a matter of eliminating the ambiguity by making oneself pure inwardness or pure externality, by escaping from the sensible world or by being engulfed in it, by yielding to eternity or enclosing oneself in the pure moment."[27] The French original reads: "il s'agissait de supprimer l'ambiguité en se faisant pure intériorité ou pure extériorité, en s'évadant du monde sensible ou en s'y engloutissant, en accédant à l'éternité ou en s'enfermant dans l'instant pur."[28]

Through the linguistic-grammatical structure of the French statements, the nature of "self" (whether or not it is substantive) is left ambiguous. In place of the "thinghood" of the self we find something closer to an activity. Following early Husserl and the Sartre who defended Husserl against Husserl, we might describe it this way: consciousness, the for-itself, is an unfolding intentional activity, and when a "self" forms out of this, as it becomes "reflective" and "reflexive" on itself, the result is a fixed structure (though very impermanently) which we call the self and conceptualize as a thing. In fact, Sartre and Beauvoir themselves conceptualize it this way. However, it would be more accurate to what early Husserl, Sartre, and Beauvoir asserted about the self to say that consciousness "selfs" itself, rather than to say that a "self" forms. This folding back upon itself is an internal action of consciousness, and the designation of the product of this activity into the English term "self"—a noun term which at least "looks like" or sounds like a thing—is misleading. The usage of the nominal form "self" would quite mistakenly "eliminate the ambiguity" (to use Beauvoir's phrase above) of the activity of consciousness, which, at some points but not at others, "selfs" itself a "self," that is, selfs itself—forms, creates, fashions, crafts itself (a "self").

In what follows, I look at aspects of Simone de Beauvoir's work that make use of these distinctions. I begin by examining her philosophical essays to investigate her allegiance to Sartrean existentialism, as well as her departures from it. It was by these departures that she formed a Beauvoirian theory that was a profound addition to earlier feminist theory. Then I will continue by examining her own autobiographical writings from this unique Beauvoirian Theory. My purpose is to find the self that she crafts for her readers and for herself.

NOTES

1. When I use the term "Other" to refer to the patriarchal status of women, I capitalize it; in discussing other "others," I use lower case ("other").

2. It should be noted that Beauvoir only *directly* argued for a particular concept of the self when she defended Sartre against Merleau-Ponty in "Merleau-Ponty et le pseudo-sartrisme," in *Privilèges* (Paris: Gallimard, 1955), pp. 203–72. This was originally published in *Les Temps modernes* 10, nos. 114–5 (June–July 1955), pp. 2072–122.

3. Herbert Spiegelberg, *The Phenomenological Movement*, 2d ed., vol. 1 (The Hague: Martinus Nijhoff, 1969), p. 87.

4. Spiegelberg, p. 714.

5. Spiegelberg, pp. 140–1.

6. See my article, "Philosophy Becomes Autobiography: the Development of the Self in the Writings of Simone de Beauvoir," in *Writing the Politics of Difference*, ed. Hugh Silverman (Albany: S.U.N.Y. Press, 1991), vol. 14 of "Selected Studies in Phenomenology and Existential Philosophy." This is my first published work on this topic.

7. Edmund Husserl, *Ideas: General Introduction to Pure Phenomenology*, trans. W. R. Boyce Gibson (New York: Collier Books, 1962), pp. 109 and 223. (*Ideas* was published in German in 1913.)

8. The notion of intentionality had been taken over by Husserl from Brentano, for whom every mental phenomenon but no physical phenomenon had intentionality, that is, a *reference* to a content; thus, "intentionality" became a way to define mental phenomena: those phenomena which include an object intentionally within themselves.

9. Jean-Paul Sartre, *The Transcendence of the Ego*, translated and annotated with an introduction by Forrest William and Robert Kirkpatrick (New York: Farrar, Straus, and Giroux, undated), p. 93. The original French version of this work appeared in 1936–7.

10. Simone de Beauvoir, *La Force de l'âge* (Paris: Gallimard, 1960), pp. 189–90. Translation mine. See Simone de Beauvoir, *The Prime of Life*, trans. Peter Green (Cleveland: World Publishing Co., 1962), pp. 147–8. Green's translation repeatedly ignores Beauvoir's philosophical terminology or confuses terms. I have chosen to use "the psyche" for her "*le psychique*"; it might be translated as "the psychic" except for the connotations of that word in English, connotations which she didn't intend. Beauvoir continued this passage by inserting a long quotation from *The Transcendence of the Ego*.

11. The problem which each tradition brings to the issue of the "self" covers some ground shared by the other tradition. A book which is most helpful in showing how these two traditions overlap on this issue is Phyllis Sutton Morris's book, *Sartre's Concept of a Person: An Analytic Approach* (Amherst: University of Massachusetts Press, 1976). Morris uses the vocabulary and questions of analytic philosophy to present Sartre's own problem to Anglo-American philosophers, making insightful comparisons and contrasts between Sartre's thought and theirs.

In a different vein, an article by Sartrean translator and scholar Hazel Barnes, "Sartre's Concept of the Self," *Review of Existential Psychology and Psychiatry* 17, no. 1 (1980–81), pp. 41–65, contains a discussion of the variety of concepts of the self Sartre uses, as well as an acknowledgment of the confusion in Sartre's terminology which makes the study of this issue so difficult.

Finding scholarship on Beauvoir can be tricky. Research in *The Philosopher's Index* under the subject "Beauvoir" will uncover the following absences and presences, noted here for the benefit of future researchers: (1) no entries in many of the volumes, (2) entries, but not under her name, nor under the titles of her works, (3) entries for whole books written solely on Beauvoir, listed only under Sartre's name, and (4) Beauvoir's name sometimes listed under "D" and sometimes under "B."

12. This Sartrean tension is incorporated in the quotation from Sartre on the frontispiece of the French edition: "*A moitiè victimes, à moitiè complices, comme tout le monde*" ("Half victims, half accomplices, like everyone"). The term "situation," an important part of the analysis Beauvoir presents in *The Second Sex*, preserves this tension well, since it carries an existential-phenomenological analysis, and avoids an essentialist one.

13. Amelie Oksenberg Rorty, Introduction, *The Identities of Persons*, ed. Amelie Oksenberg Rorty (Berkeley: University of California Press, 1976), pp. 1–15.

14. Rorty, pp. 10–11.

15. Rorty, p. 11.

16. Martin Heidegger, *Being and Time*, trans. John Macquarrie and Edward Robinson (New York: Harper and Row, 1962), p. 32.

17. Rorty, p. 13.

18. Rorty, p. 15.

19. Amelie Oksenberg Rorty, "A Literary Postscript: Characters, Persons, Selves, Individuals," in *The Identities of Persons*, pp. 309–17.

20. Rorty, p. 317.

21. Charles Taylor, "Responsibility for Self," in Rorty, p. 281.

22. Taylor, p. 282.

23. Taylor, p. 299.

24. John H. Brueckner, compiler and editor, *Brueckner's French Contextuary* (Englewood Cliffs, NJ: Prentice-Hall, 1975), p. 381.

25. Simone de Beauvoir, *The Ethics of Ambiguity*, trans. Bernard Frechtman (New York: Citadel Press, 1970), p. 8. (Hereafter, *Ethics*.)

26. *Ethics*, p. 8.

27. *Ethics*, p. 8.

28. Simone de Beauvoir, *Pour une morale de l'ambiguité* (Paris: Editions Gallimard, 1974), pp. 10–11.

1

Self and Other in Beauvoir's Early Essays

Though she is commonly judged to be one of the foremost exponents of French existentialism, Beauvoir's own philosophical creativity was overshadowed by her connection to Sartre during much of her lifetime. She was partially responsible for that; at numerous places in her autobiography she denied her own creativity and any significant interest in philosophy as her life's work, and insisted on Sartre's philosophical preeminence over her. She also took up the defense of his ideas on more than one occasion, as in "Merleau-Ponty et le pseudo-sartrisme," once describing it as a job that "any Sartrean" could have done.[1] Many scholars, biographers, and critics of her work interpret her in this manner. Others (feminist philosophers in particular) have tried, in spite of Beauvoir's own assertions, to establish a claim of her philosophical autonomy from Sartre's thought, as well as begin the discussion of the influence of her thinking upon his. This latter is a point of view on Beauvoir which most of her biographers and scholars have ignored.[2] Thus, the Beauvoir scholar is faced with what might be called Beauvoir's "Sartrean exterior," particularly in her specifically philosophical writings. In this chapter, I cover some of the ground of that Sartrean exterior, while acknowledging her innovative moves in *The Ethics of Ambiguity*. In the next chapter, "Self and Other in *The Second Sex*," I will study her most dramatic move away from Sartrean existentialism, her analysis of woman as Other.

PYRRHUS ET CINÉAS

The essay *Pyrrhus et Cinéas*, published in 1944 and still not translated into English, was Beauvoir's first published philosophical work. After the novel *The Blood of Others,* it was the second work of what she termed her "moral period."[3] The essay takes its title from a story told by Plutarch of a conversation between Pyrrhus, one of the greatest generals in antiquity, about to embark on yet another military campaign, and Cinéas, his trusted lieutenant, who advises against the new campaign. When she relates the old story, Beauvoir acknowledges that, in the conventional interpretation of this story, Cinéas is in the right, since it seems wise not to leave home, only to return one day.[4] But Beauvoir defends Pyrrhus, using him as a prototype of the existentialist hero: "Man only exists in choosing himself; if he refuses to choose, he annihilates himself."[5] Pyrrhus's military adventurism is a form of activism and is better than indifference or inactivity, as Beauvoir sees it.[6] The two figures, Pyrrhus and Cinéas, become symbols of the active and passive aspects of the for-itself, the human subject. At this stage, Beauvoir used the term "subjectivity" to indicate the active component of the self, that is, the for-itself:

because my subjectivity isn't inert, folding back on itself (*sur soi*), separation, but on the contrary, movement toward the other . . . the difference between the other and me is abolished . . . the bond that unites me to the other only I alone (*moi seul*) can create . . . from the fact that I am not a thing but a project of myself toward the other, a transcendence.[7]

The self as for-itself, as subject, is not a thing; further, by its projection through actions, its "transcendence," the self creates a bond with others. Movement toward the other is exemplified in certain choices that one makes to value the other; thus, concretely and specifically, *a posteriori*, not *a priori,* the self finds others valuable because it makes them valuable through its own actions in regard to them.

Beauvoir pointedly uses the Sartrean term "project" (*projet*) in this passage; she combines it with the Heideggerian notion of "thrownness," but also adds to these her own emphasis on the other to create a uniquely Beauvoirian notion of the self:

It's not *for* the other that each transcends oneself; one writes books . . . invents machines . . . craved nowhere; nor is this for the self (*pour soi*) because "self" (*soi*) exists only through the same project which throws one into the world . . . we need the other so that our existence becomes established and necessary. . . . My acts, my works, my life: it's only by these objects that I make . . . that I can communicate with the other.[8]

Beauvoir further develops her notion of the human being as for-itself through an argument with Heidegger, specifically against his notion that *Dasein* is being-towards-death.[9] Heidegger argued in *Being and Time* that death, as the end of *Dasein,* was *Dasein's* "ownmost possibility"; thus an "authentic" life would necessitate an acceptance of death by *expecting* it: "the more . . . this possibility gets understood, the more purely does the understanding penetrate into it *as the possibility of the impossibility of any existence at all. . . .* [in this way] Being-towards-death is the anticipation of a potentiality-for-Being of that entity whose kind of Being is anticipation itself."[10] This anticipation is essentially anxiety, and the experience of that anxiety, the self-understanding that it exhibits, is the sign of authentic existence.[11]

Even though Heidegger argued against the notion of human interiority, Beauvoir claims here that his insistence that authentic *Dasein* is being-towards-death amounts to a claim of the interiority or immanence of the human being. She maintained that one needn't accept Heidegger's contention that being-towards-death is *the* human project, or "that death is our ownmost possibility (*notre fin essentielle*)."[12] For Heidegger, the project of being-towards-death was the only authentic project; this amounted to a definition by limitation of the human being. Yet, Beauvoir claimed, to delimit it is to deny its transcendence, to fix it into a preassigned mold: "The nothingness that angst reveals to me isn't the nothingness of my death; it is, in the heart of my life, the negativity that permits me to transcend."[13] Because Heidegger's claim translated to an assertion that authentic subjectivity is a type of thinghood—an immanence, not a transcendence—it is mistaken. Subjectivity is not immanence; it is transcendence, an engagement in the world. In arguing this, Beauvoir rejects the notion that the human subject has transcendence of a particular type or meaning, a kind of "stability" of self, given through the one particular and overarching project of being-towards-death, within which all other projects are subsumed and all transcendence enveloped.

In making this criticism of Heidegger, Beauvoir was reiterating, to some extent, Sartre's argument near the end of *Being and Nothingness,* in which he insisted that being-towards-death would not be an "authentic project" for every person, since each person has her or his own original, fundamental project, which was the original choice of each individual's own being:

We cannot stop at those classifications of "authentic project" and "unauthentic project of the self" which Heidegger wished to establish. . . . Consequently anguish (anxiety) before death and resolute decision or flight into unauthenticity cannot be considered as fundamental projects of our being. On the contrary, they can be understood only on the foundation of an original project of *living*; that is, on an original choice of our being. It is right then in each case to pass beyond the results of Heidegger's interpretation toward a still more fundamental project . . . the original project of a for-itself *can aim only at its being.*

THE ETHICS OF AMBIGUITY

In 1947, Beauvoir published her well-known philosophical work, *The Ethics of Ambiguity*, her attempt to create an ethics based on the analysis of human existence presented in Sartre's *Being and Nothingness*.[14] In this work she follows the Sartrean distinction between being-for-itself (intentional being, human existence) and being-in-itself. Sartre's for-itself is free, that is, defined in its core as freedom, and because it is nothing, it is not determined. In this Sartrean analysis, the freedom that the for-itself has and is moves toward the future, choosing and pursuing ideals—"projects." In so doing, the for-itself transcends or surpasses itself; each goal achieved or failed becomes a new point of departure for a new moment of the self. This means that to be a "self," that is, a for-itself, a being with transcendence, is already to be free. Beauvoir follows Sartre's notion that the transcendence of the for-itself is a negativity; "the for-itself carries nothingness in its heart," she says.[15]   Beginning with these basic elements of Sartrean ontology, Beauvoir constructed her ethics.

In that it is a nothingness, a negativity rather than a substance, the for-itself is marked by a particular characteristic, one that becomes the central concept of Beauvoir's ethics: ambiguity. Ambiguity becomes synonymous with the freedom of the for-itself; for Beauvoir, it is the mark of the human condition. This foregrounds the existentialist claim that human life is never fixed (i.e., has no nature); individuals neither participate in a universal human nature nor have an individual, fixed nature. Human existence is ambiguous—uncertain and undefined.   Hence, failure *is* possible. It is in this sense that Beauvoir claims that the for-itself does not "coincide" with itself. Without the possibility of failure, ethics itself is impossible, she says, since for any being which is in "exact co-incidence" with itself, the ethical "ought," that is, "having-to-be," is meaningless.[16] Similar to Heidegger's claim that the self is "at a distance" from itself, this is also the claim of a "lack of being" of which Sartre spoke. Here the negativity of the for-itself emerges, since it is nothing, has no nature, no content, but is only a distancing, a movement of transcendence. Beauvoir says this negativity is a sign of "intentionality," a term laden with phenomenological significance: "This lack of being [is] *in order that* there might be being . . . '*in order that*' clearly indicates an intentionality . . . [by which] being is disclosed . . . 'wanting to disclose being'—now, here there is not failure, but rather success."[17]

But this "lack of being," which is freedom, can be felt either positively or negatively. Beauvoir describes a set of "archetypes" of human existence: the sub-man, the serious man, the nihilist, the adventurer, the passionate man; these can be seen also as stages, so to speak, on the way to the achievement of an ethical life. She distinguishes them by the manner in which each experiences the ambiguity of existence. For the nihilist, the ambiguity of existence is not experienced positively as freedom or transcendence, but is rather seen merely as a lack. The nihilist's challenge to all given values never allows for an acknowledgment of human freedom. Given that "the world *possesses* no justification" and that "the self *is* nothing," the nihilist forgets that the justification of the world and the existence of the self depend on human activity.[18] The adventurer, by contrast, experiences this ambiguity positively. Through the adventurer's continual and deliberate choice-making and setting of new goals, she or he acknowledges human freedom. Though neither nihilists nor adventurers accept or are resigned to given values, the adventurer knows that beyond the simple and nihilistic refusal of specific "givens" there is the ongoing acceptance of human freedom itself, as manifested in one's ongoing choices. But the quality that prevents the adventurer from being the ethical hero highlights an important element in Beauvoir's ethics. In her judgment, adventurism paints a solipsistic and unrealistic world, since "every Don Juan is confronted with Elviras"—that is, our actions take place in a human world and produce human consequences.[19] In contrast to adventurism, Beauvoirian existentialism insists on the centrality of the me-others bond and is radically nonsolipsistic and radically nonindividualistic.

The for-itself also desires its own objectification; it wants to be in-itself, a thing, or more completely, God, the "in-itself-for-itself," as Sartre had put it. But neither the objectification of thinghood nor that of divinity are possible for the for-itself, so this desire is doomed to failure. An additional desire of the for-itself to disclose being, which equates to the intentionality of consciousness, manifests itself. By the disclosure of being, the disclosure of the world, the for-itself acknowledges its negativity and accepts itself as lack of being.[20]

Through Beauvoir's interpretation, this ontological description becomes a moral imperative; the descriptive analysis turns doubly prescriptive. First she claims that the self should take up or "assume" its negativity—its distance from itself—and in so doing, it will assume its freedom and be ethical. Beauvoir compares this, which she calls the "existentialist conversion," to the Husserlian practice of reduction. Without attempting to deny and ignore the ambiguity of the human condition, one puts the "will to be 'in parentheses'" to realize the truth of the human situation.[21] Further, it should seek, through choices of values and projects, to "ground itself," to take up its freedom through concrete means.[22] To will one's freedom in concrete ways is to become moral—to accept and not flee from that nothingness that humans are. By contrast, to refuse to accept it or, worse, to hinder the freedom of others is to be immoral.

Though the individual subject is sovereign and unique, an absolute, the sovereignty of the subject can be "disturbed" in two ways. Both disturbances have to do with the existence of other people, as themselves subjects and as part of a collectivity of human beings. First, the subject can also be an object for others.[23] Second, the subject, though it is an individual, is also a "*mitsein*" (a notion not original to Beauvoir), a being-with-others.

By combining these two "disturbances" of subjectivity, Beauvoir makes a claim that is a significant addition to the existential-phenomenological ontology of Sartre that she began with. As she puts it, "the me-other relationship is as indissoluble as the subject-object relationship."[24] She begins with the axiom that human subjectivity, the for-itself, is active, always moving toward a project. But she adds to the Sartrean ontology two important notions: first, that subjectivity requires justification; and second, that it receives it in the existence of other human beings. The human being seeks an answer to the question that arises from existential anxiety: how can one, or *can* one, explain or defend one's existence or validate the fact that one "finds oneself" here, without explanation, without excuse (Heidegger's notion of "thrownness")? The answer is that the *only* form in which such justification comes is through the existence of others: "I concern others and they concern me," she says.[25] (She does not provide extended arguments for these points in *The Ethics of Ambiguity*, but she does note that she had argued for them in *Pyrrhus et Cinéas*. She may also have assumed that these extended arguments weren't necessary here, since *Being and Nothingness* contained them.) Her conclusion and "irreducible truth" is that the relation between one's self and others is an indissoluble one.[26] Since self and other are bound together ontologically, the willing of my own freedom—the for-itself's affirmatively taking on its own freedom—becomes the willing of the freedom of others. The radical individuality of the subject in Beauvoir's ethics is combined throughout with a notion that the individual exists within a collectivity; to her, this is "an irreducible truth," for "the me-others relationship is as indissoluble as the subject-object relationship. . . . To will oneself free is also to will others free."[27] Sartre had argued that the freedom of the for-itself is at once also being-for-others.[28] But in Beauvoir's analysis, the ontological claim is transformed into an ethical one: the ethics of ambiguity requires that the for-itself *will* the disclosure of being which it *is*, but which it may, in a positively moral attitude, *will*. This willing of the disclosure of being is the willing of freedom, the freedom of others as well as my own.[29] Though existentialism asserted that the self was constituted by freedom, in fact *was* freedom, the willing of freedom amounts to an assumption of it, a conscious decision not to flee it, but rather to face freedom, including the anguish and risks that freedom creates.[30]

In the existentialist problem called upon by *The Ethics of Ambiguity*, the for-itself's transcendence is tempered by its facticity. An ontological system which rejects determinism and virtually equates the human being with freedom, as did Sartrean existentialism, must make at least some concession to the hindrances or resistances which freedom encounters; these factors provide a "coefficient of adversity" to the freedom of the for-itself;[31] they include one's place, one's body, one's past, one's general environment, other human beings, and one's death.[32]

Beauvoir's famous claim that "ethics is the triumph of freedom over facticity" was meant to incorporate political issues into her existentialist ethics, an incorporation seen in several of her novels as well.[33] Those forces which deny human freedom also attempt to turn the human being into mere facticity, "a thing among things."[34] Such "parties of oppression" who perform this reduction of others to immanence, to pure facticity, use that very reduction to claim that those they oppress are *only* facticity, only immanence, in order to validate the torture or destruction they perform against them.[35] In making this point, Beauvoir uses the victims of the Holocaust, as well as those of French colonialism in Algeria, as examples of those who are victimized by tyrannical attempts to reduce the for-itself to an in-itself, to reduce human existence to its facticity and ignore its freedom. In asserting their own transcendence, these parties of oppression immorally and violently force others into immanence, in spite of the fact that the human being is "a being of the distances, a movement toward the future."[36] Because such oppressors are intent on turning transcendence into mere immanence, their freedom is the only freedom *not* deserving of respect, she says.

But *The Ethics of Ambiguity* served to introduce claims and problems that Beauvoir would use later in *The Second Sex* and issues that she would return to in her autobiography: the other, one's bond with the other, responsibility to the other, and further, the problems imposed by these very bonds—for though "to will oneself free is also to will others free," others are "separate, even opposed" to the self.[37] When she turned her attention to women's situation, she found herself one of the "others" more than she ever thought possible; in that analysis, she asserts that woman is the absolute Other for the patriarchal era.

"L'EXISTENTIALISME ET LA SAGESSE DES NATIONS"

In 1948, in an article in *L'Existentialisme et la sagesse des nations*, a work consisting of four essays, Beauvoir was at pains to defend existentialism, as well as to emphasize the importance of the for-itself, a term she used interchangeably with "subjectivity."[38] In the title essay, her explanation revolves around the difference between philosophies (and psychologies) of immanence which consider the self—the "me" or ego—to be a thinglike construction, and existentialism, a philosophy of existence: "For existentialism the 'me' doesn't exist; I exist as authentic subject, in a springing forth that is ceaselessly renewed which opposes itself to the fixed reality of things," she said.[39] Thus, the self and the for-itself are mutually exclusive. Existentialism's claim of the importance of subjectivity is equated with the definition of the human being as transcendence. The self as for-itself, subject, not the self as ego, is engagement in the world and also movement toward the other; in contrast, the self posited by philosophies of immanence is one to whom all actions and feelings of the human being turn back. In this latter view, no active subject appears, but a "self" (*moi*), as object in the world, and from this object one's behavior stems, for "if one can love her self (*moi*), to accept it as a pole of her conduct, it's because it exists the way a thing exists," Beauvoir says.[40] This immanent self has needs which are to be satisfied; in fact, its demands may swallow up one's freedom: "my self (*moi*) imposes on me objective aims . . . it's necessary that I satisfy its needs, that I procure it the pleasures it desires, that I protect it against suffering."[41] Because the self was a conceptual burden that sullied the claim of the radical freedom of the for-itself, existentialism mistrusted it. At this point in her thinking, Beauvoir interpreted existentialism as a philosophy which indisputably denied the self (the "me" or ego) by affirming a notion of subjectivity that allowed for the individual's choices, but not its needs. In *The Transcendence of the Ego*, Sartre had said that there indeed was an ego, but that it was not *inside* consciousness but external to it, as is any object. In order to affirm that consciousness is subjectivity, Beauvoir stressed the importance of the for-itself, still remaining wary of the self.

However, Beauvoir's notion of the self operates in *both* the traditions of existentialism and phenomenology. She seemed unaware of the questionable meldings that were required to join these two schools; in this she was not alone. For existentialist philosophy, there is a subject; subjectivity is central. In fact, truth itself is equated with a subjectivity (the thinking of the early existentialists Kierkegaard and Nietzsche bears this out best). The self ("*le moi*") doesn't exist; it is part of the baggage of philosophies of immanence which claim human existence has the status of the *en-soi*. To claim selfhood is to claim thinghood. Beauvoir's essays of the later forties explain and defend existentialism, this philosophy of subjectivity. This position was held by others, as well as by Sartre and Beauvoir; for example, Gabriel Marcel, who also distinguished the subject from the empirical, determined "I."[42]

By contrast, for phenomenology, the self as the I, ego, does exist, but only as a product of consciousness. But the status of subjectivity is questionable. Herbert Spiegelberg's interpretation is that the "older" phenomenological movement (i.e., pre-Husserl) was actually "antisubjectivistic," an emphasis later changed to some extent by Husserl and elaborated upon by Sartre.[43]

"MERLEAU-PONTY ET LE PSEUDO-SARTRISME"

In an important but neglected essay by Beauvoir, "Merleau-Ponty et le pseudo-sartrisme," the problems of the coexistence of existentialism and phenomenology which were operating in *The Second Sex* become apparent. Though "Merleau-Ponty et le pseudo-sartrisme" was written several years after *The Second Sex*, Beauvoir incorporated none of its lessons within the essay. It is an apologia for Sartre and a strong attack on Merleau-Ponty, her once-close friend, who was also the working colleague of both Sartre and herself on the editorial board of the journal *Les Temps modernes*. In this essay, Beauvoir categorically rejects Merleau-Ponty's reading of Sartrean philosophy, which she labels a "flagrant" falsification, because it claims that Sartrism is a "philosophy of the subject."[44] In her rejection of Merleau-Ponty's "Sartrism," she clarifies the boundaries between existentialism and phenomenology.

Existentialism is a philosophy that stresses the individual and asserts the primacy of the individual's ability to make choices and to make one's "self." It claimed a primary place for freedom. Though Sartre did acknowledge the importance of facticity, though he insisted that "existence" was the conjunction of freedom and facticity, freedom became his focus. The phenomenological school, on the other hand, expounded a new sort of positivity, the description of the appearances, or "profiles," of objects by intuitive acts of consciousness. These descriptions were not said to be factual, or descriptions of "facticity"; they derived meaning from acts of consciousness. So phenomenology attempted to go beyond the dualism that Sartre's "freedom vs. facticity" distinction still used. Whereas Sartre had said human beings were "condemned" to be free, Merleau-Ponty said that human beings were "condemned" to meaning.

In Beauvoir's view, it is not Sartrism but "Pseudo-Sartrism" which is a "philosophy of the subject," that is, a philosophy that mistakenly equates "consciousness" with "subject," that emphasizes the importance of the subject over the world and others; whereas "true Sartrism" is a philosophy of consciousness, and not of the subject. Pseudo-Sartrism assumes that there is a "sense" given or imposed on things by a "decree" of consciousness, that the world and the things of the world hold no meaning other than what consciousness provides to them. In addition, it holds the existence of the other as unimportant, because the other is seen as just another object under the "gaze" of the subject: "The existence of the other doesn't break this 'tete-a-tete' because the other only appears under the figure of another subject; the relation of I and other dimishes in the gaze; each one lives alone in the heart of his own universe upon which he reigns as sovereign; there is no need of an intermundane space."[45] In Sartrean ontology correctly understood, consciousness is identical to the pure, immediate presence to self; it is "for-itself," while the "subject" is the "ego," the "*soi*," the self. Consciousness is immediate presence to itself (*à soi*).

This self, the ego, is a "transcendent" being. Thus it appears as an object to and for consciousness, that is, it is intended, not intending: "The psyche and the Me (*le Moi*) which is its pole are intended by consciousness as objects. Merleau-Ponty has forgotten this fundamental thesis when he claims: 'Sartre said that there is no difference between an imaginary love and a true love because the subject is by definition what he thinks himself to be.'"[46] Consciousness, on the other hand, is immediate presence to self (*à soi*); it is, or carries, the mechanism of intentionality. The self is not within consciousness, but in the "distance," as object. Differently stated, this assertion claims that one's consciousness is immediate presence to self, whereas one's subjectivity, the existence of oneself as a subject, requires mediation. The subject and the world reciprocally disclose each other.[47]

Merleau-Ponty's conception of the Sartrean notion of consciousness was that it is co-constitutive of meaning, an actual opposite and coequal to the world—in Merleau-Ponty's phrase, "coextensive to the world." The self is that immanence, that totality, which the for-itself lacks. Merleau-Ponty had claimed that Sartre felt that the subject held a "mastery," a sovereignty, over the world, rather than a partnership with it. In refuting this, Beauvoir insisted that the subject is not *within* consciousness, but is an object to it:

Sartre has always insisted on the reciprocal conditioning of the world and the self (*le Moi*). "Without the world, no ipseity, no person: without ipseity, without the person, no world." . . . This is what Sartre calls "the circuit of selfness (ipseity)" and this idea is radically opposed to that which Merleau-Ponty takes when he points out with a useless good sense that "the subject isn't the sun from whence the world shines, the demigod of our pure objects."[48]

The subject is a "transcendent" and not a "transcendental," hence, it is an object that can be surpassed, transcended, through the freedom of consciousness. One is "stuck" with one's consciousness, but not with one's subjectivity, not with one's selfness.

In essence, in this essay Beauvoir claimed that Merleau-Ponty set up a straw man in his attack on Sartre. He and Sartre agree, as does she, on the secondary importance of the *subject*, the nonoriginary nature of it, and the coequal status of the *world* and *consciousness*.[49] Nevertheless, in her defense of Sartre she inadvertently pointed to a weakness in existentialism that had become apparent in *The Second Sex,* a work in which the importance of freedom relative to facticity had shifted. Yet in the "Merleau-Ponty" essay, she resolutely maintained that facticity had been important (already) in Sartrean ontology:

What Merleau-Ponty neglects here is the theory of *facticity* which is one of the bases of the Sartrean ontology. My consciousness can't surpass the world that engages it, that is, in condemning itself to understand [the world] in a univocal and finished perspective, to be infinitely and without recourse projected by it; and this is why there is only incarnated consciousness. . . . Surpassing the world is specifically not to fly over it; it is to engage oneself in it in order to emerge from it.[50]

Regardless of Beauvoir's protestations, it is fair to say that Merleau-Ponty's reaction to Sartre's political writing (which was the reason for this essay) was a fitting response to the relative unimportance of facticity in Sartrean existentialism. Though Sartre had given facticity a place in his thinking, he nevertheless presented it as the poor stepsister to freedom.

NOTES

1. Simone de Beauvoir, *Force of Circumstance*, trans. Richard Howard (New York: Harper Colophon Books, 1977), p. 318. (Hereafter, *Force.*) "Any Sartrean had the right to defend a philosophy that he had made his own," Beauvoir said.

2. Several new books that have appeared recently are turning the tide, and giving Beauvoir her philosophical due: Kate and Edward Fullbrook, *Simone de Beauvoir and Jean-Paul Sartre: The Remaking of a Twentieth-Century Legend* (New York: HarperCollins, 1994); Margaret A. Simons, ed., *Feminist Interpretations of Simone de Beauvoir* (University Park: The Pennsylvania State University Press, 1995); and

Debra B. Bergoffen, *The Philosophy of Simone de Beauvoir: Gendered Phenomenologies, Erotic Generosities* (Albany: S.U.N.Y. Press, 1997), a book that I have not yet read, as this goes to press.

3. She used this term in her second work of autobiography; see Simone de Beauvoir, *The Prime of Life*, trans. Peter Green (Cleveland: World Publishing/Meridian Books, 1966), p. 433.

4. Simone de Beauvoir, *Pyrrhus et Cinéas* (Paris: Gallimard, 1944), p. 9. All translations for this essay are mine. (Hereafter, *PC.*)

5. *PC*, p. 60.

6. Beauvoir here leads one to believe that if Pyrrhus hadn't gone to another war, he would be living a life without making choices. She somewhat sarcastically comments on Candide's remark, "We must cultivate our garden." "What is our garden?" she asks. One could respond, "and what is action?" Pyrrhus could also have stayed at home and "cultivated his garden" in some nonmilitary fashion with the money he spent on the military campaign. *PC*, p. 11.

7. *PC*, p. 16.

8. *PC*, pp. 96–7.

9. The French translator of Heidegger's *Being and Time*, Corbin, used *la réalité humaine* (human reality) for *Dasein*, terminology which Sartre often uses.

10. Martin Heidegger, *Being and Time*, trans. John Macquarrie and Edward Robinson (New York: Harper and Row, 1962), p. 307.

11. Heidegger, p. 310.

12. *PC*, pp. 61–2.

13. *PC*, p. 63.

14. Simone de Beauvoir, *The Ethics of Ambiguity*, trans. Bernard Frechtman (New York: Citadel Press, 1970), pp. 10–11. (Hereafter, *Ethics.*) For her direct comments on the circumstances of the writing of this and on her own evaluation of it, see *Force*, pp. 66–8.

15. *Ethics*, p. 31.

16. *Ethics*, p. 10. See also Sartre, *Being and Nothingness*, p. 96, passim.

17. *Ethics*, p. 12.

18. *Ethics*, p. 57.

19. *Ethics*, p. 60.

20. *Ethics*, p. 12, passim.

21. *Ethics*, pp. 13–4.

22. *Ethics*, p. 16.

23. This point was originally derived by the French existentialists from Hegel's "master-slave dialectic" in his *Phenomenology of Spirit*. G.W.F. Hegel, *The Phenomenology of Mind*, trans. J.B. Baillie (London: George Allen & Unwin LTD, 1964), pp. 228–40.

24. *Ethics*, pp. 72–3.

25. *Ethics*, p. 72.

26. *Ethics*, p. 72.

27. *Ethics*, pp. 72–3.

28. Sartre had analyzed the for-itself according to these three *ekstases*: (1) the

tridimensional one of temporality, (2) the reflective *ekstasis*, and (3) the *ekstasis* of the for-itself as being-for-others. See *Being and Nothingness*, pp. 395–400.

29. *Ethics*, pp. 73 and 135.

30. *Ethics*, p. 34.

31. See Glossary in Sartre, *Being and Nothingness*.

32. Sartre, *Being and Nothingness*, pp. 599–677.

33. *Ethics*, p. 44, passim.

34. *Ethics*, p. 100.

35. *Ethics*, p. 99.

36. *Ethics*, p. 100.

37. *Ethics*, p. 73.

38. Simone de Beauvoir, *L'Existentialisme et la sagesse des nations* (Paris: Editions Nagel, 1963). This was originally published in 1948; it has never been translated into English. Terry Keefe, in his *Simone de Beauvoir: A Study of Her Writings* (Totowa, NJ: Barnes and Noble Books, 1983), p. 87, says that these essays were first published in *Les Temps modernes* and actually predate *Ethics*.

39. "L'Existentialisme et la sagesse des nations," in *L'Existentialisme et la sagesse des nations*, p. 36.

40. "Existentialisme," p. 35.

41. "Existentialisme," pp. 35–6.

42. Gabriel Marcel, "An Essay in Autobiography," in *The Philosophy of Existentialism* (New York: Citadel Press, 1956), p. 120.

43. Herbert Spiegelberg, *The Phenomenological Movement*, 2d ed., vol. 1(The Hague: Martinus Nijhoff, 1969), p. 666.

44. Simone de Beauvoir, "Merleau-Ponty et le pseudo-sartrisme," in *Privilèges* (Paris: Gallimard, 1955), p. 209. This was originally published in *Les Temps modernes* and has only recently been been translated into English (in an issue of *International Studies in Philosophy*), but I use my own translation throughout. The title is formed from a wordplay on Merleau-Ponty's piece, "Sartre et l'ultra-bolchevisme," chapter 5 in Merleau-Ponty's *Adventures of the Dialectic*, a response to Sartre's *The Communists and Peace*. See *Force*, pp. 318–9, for her complete discussion of this.

45. "Merleau-Ponty," p. 205.

46. "Merleau-Ponty," p. 205. Beauvoir is here quoting Merleau-Ponty's *Aventures de la Dialectique*.

47. Sartre, *Being and Nothingness*, pp. 126–8.

48. "Merleau-Ponty," p. 206.

49. "Merleau-Ponty," p. 206. In this passage, the cluster of terms she exchanges for "subject" is extensive, including "*moi*" (me), "*je*" (I), "*ego*," "*psyche*," "*soi*" (self), and "*personne*"; these terms can be substituted for each other by and large, and they are radically distinguished from "consciousness." Beauvoir overlooked a distinction Sartre made, however. Though he does claim that "consciousness" does not equal "subject" or "self," he does want to retain a labored distinction between "subject" and "self." See Sartre, *Being and Nothingness*, pp. 93–4.

50. "Merleau-Ponty," pp. 206–7.

2

Self and Other in *The Second Sex*

In her autobiography, relating the beginnings of the intellectual project that resulted in *The Second Sex*, Beauvoir tells us that, though she wanted to write an autobiography, she decided to question first the importance of her gender to her individual life: "I wanted to write about myself. . . . I realized that the first question to come up was: What has it meant to me to be a woman?"[1] She then turned to the project that became *The Second Sex*:

I looked, and it was a revelation: this world was a masculine world, my childhood had been nourished by myths forged by men, and I hadn't reacted to them in at all the same way I should have done if I had been a boy. I was so interested . . . that I abandoned my project for a personal confession in order to give all my attention to finding out about the condition of woman in its broadest terms. I went to the Bibliothèque Nationale to do some reading, and what I studied were the myths of femininity.[2]

Later, discussing its reception, Beauvoir said that the book's contents were distorted and the distorted ideas were attributed to her. She became the object of sarcastic attack, her sexuality publicly impugned, her morality questioned, her personhood supposedly "humiliated" by her writing—attacked both by those she would have expected and by those she never expected. She was flabbergasted at the strength of opposition the book unleashed and at the personal nature of the attacks.[3]

Published in two volumes in French, the entire work is initiated with an introduction (now a classic in its own right) and ends with a conclusion; each volume is organized into parts: four in the first one and three in the second. Within these parts, Beauvoir uses a number of theoretical approaches. She mixes theories of human psychological development with theories of historical materialism, anthropological theory, existentialism, phenomenology, and Hegelianism.

The philosophical problem posed in *The Second Sex* is clearly stated on the first page of the Introduction, when Beauvoir forcefully claims, "first we must ask: what is a woman?"[4] As the Introduction progresses, Beauvoir gives this answer: woman is the Other.[5] Woman *is* the Other, but woman is *not* the Other. The paradox is only resolved by a Hegelian reading:

> when an individual (or a group of individuals) is kept in a situation of inferiority, the fact is that he *is* inferior. But . . . the verb *to be* must be rightly understood here; it is in bad faith to give it a static value when it really has the dynamic Hegelian sense of "to have become." Yes, women on the whole *are* today inferior to men; that is, their situation affords them fewer possibilities.[6]

In order to arrive at her notion of woman as the Other, Beauvoir had to begin by arguing against two major philosophic traditions. The first is the tradition she calls "conceptualism," which claims that universals such as "woman" exist. This tradition becomes identified with "essentialism," or the notion that things have essences which are permanently fixed. Beauvoir notes that something called "femininity" is presumed to be the "essence" of "woman"; to some philosophers this "femininity" has been identical with anatomy, for example, by those who claim that "*tota mulier in utero*," that is, "woman is a womb."[7] The second is the tradition she calls "nominalism," specifically that branch of it connected to the rationalist tradition of the enlightenment, which insists on the equation of all human beings as human beings, and which claims there are no essential differences in them, but that all differences are merely conventions set up through language. She argues against this because, in its assertion that all meaning can be reduced to the fact of "labeling," it ignores both the causes and effects of the labeling. It ignores as well the many ways in which societies use these distinctions to create meaning and, by doing this, perpetuate certain power relations.

Early in the Introduction, Beauvoir dismissed conceptualism by calling on the evidence of the biological and social sciences which, she said, "no longer admit the existence of unchangeably fixed entities . . . [since] science regards any characteristic as a reaction dependent in part upon a *situation*."[8] It's surprising that an existentialist would use the authority of the sciences, specifically to provide evidence. Should we assume this is merely a rhetorical device? Yet Beauvoir derives the term "situation," which she repeatedly calls upon throughout the book, from science, not from existentialist philosophy. In the Introduction to Book Two, she reiterates this dismissal of conceptualism when she says, "When I use the words *woman* or *feminine* I evidently refer to no archetype, no changeless essence whatever; the reader must understand the phrase 'in the present state of education and custom' after most of my statements."[9]

Secondly, she rejects nominalism, a philosophy which claims that there are no differences among people—that all people can only be defined as human beings and not through any other qualities, since in some ways people are alike, so that all are ultimately reducible to the category, "human beings." This rejection is done with little argument, and again, on the basis of empirical, if not "scientific," evidence: "to go for a walk with one's eyes open is enough to demonstrate that humanity is divided into two classes of individuals whose clothes, faces, bodies, smiles, gaits, interests, and occupations are manifestly different" and whether "these differences are superficial" and "destined to disappear . . . right now they do most obviously exist."[10] The nominalist position, to deny that *women* exist, is inadequate, an abstract simplification, she insists, and "a flight from reality."[11] Her dismissal of conceptualism on the one hand, because of the formal evidence of the sciences ("the biological and social sciences no longer admit the existence of unchangeably fixed entities"), and nominalism on the other hand, because of the informal empirical evidence of the senses ("to go for a walk with one's eyes open"), prepares the reader to accept Beauvoir's radical theory: that woman is "defined and differentiated with reference to man and not he with reference to her; she is the incidental, the inessential as opposed to the essential. He is the Subject, he is the Absolute—she is the Other."[12]

When Beauvoir names the sickness of the patriarchal era as the notion of woman as Other, she has arrived at her first answer to the original problem posed: what is a woman? A woman is the Other. By the end of the Introduction, the cure for the sickness is announced: it is existentialist ethics. Only a philosophy like existentialism, which acknowledges the importance of the freedom of the subject, can provide us with an understanding of the seriousness of the affliction of Otherness for woman, in which a subject is forced to be an object, an existential state in which the woman's own transcendence is "overshadowed and forever transcended by another ego" which insists on its own essentiality and sovereignty.[13] Here she provides the second answer to the question: what is a woman? A woman is *not* the Other, though woman has become the Other. The Hegelian reading mentioned earlier allows her to acknowledge that, though the answer of conceptualism to the question "what is a woman?" would be that "woman is the Other, essentially, eternally," the answer of an existentialism derived from Hegelianism would be that woman is Other—but not essentially and eternally, though woman has become Other.

Scholars (for example, Michèle LeDoeuff) have noted that, in order to use existentialism in *The Second Sex*, Beauvoir had to overcome certain aspects of it that were limitations to her project.[14] The book mixes a great deal of empirical data with the freedom of the for-itself to the oppression of women and hence places great emphasis on woman's situation and condition. As a spokesperson for a philosophy which focused on the individual and the freedom of the individual, she ran the risk of being accused of validating determinism, which runs counter to the existentialist notion of the human being, particularly the early form of Sartrean existentialism; "man is free, man *is* freedom," Sartre had written in "Existentialism Is a Humanism," in 1946.[15]

The Second Sex is a work which is certainly existentialist in approach and by announcement, yet Beauvoir combined other theories with existentialism, thereby diluting the existentialist ontology that she continually calls upon throughout the book.[16] It was primarily the theories of Hegel and Levi-Strauss (the latter's theory soon to be called structuralism) that she added to existentialism to create the Beauvoirian analysis we find in *The Second Sex*, sometimes called "existential feminism." That term is a bit misleading, since existentialism is only one of the theoretical strands Beauvoir used in the book. This point is obvious in the Introduction, in which Beauvoir sets out the theoretical foundations for the work, and it continues to be obvious throughout at numerous junctures in the main text. Beauvoir specifically notes the need to use Hegelian categories *and* Levi-Straussian structuralism. Levi-Strauss's newest research was made available to her by the author (whom she knew) in manuscript form, and it became critical to her argument in the Introduction, particularly his claim that humanity's progression from Nature to Culture is distinguished by the ability to see relations in the biological realm as opposites. But this "series of contrasts: duality, alternation, opposition, and symmetry," she argued, though "fundamental . . . data of social reality," remains a mystery, if we assume that "human society were simply a *Mitsein* or fellowship based on solidarity and friendliness"; rather, "things become clear . . . if following Hegel, we find in consciousness itself a fundamental hostility toward every other consciousness; the subject can be posed only in being opposed—he sets himself up as the essential, as opposed to the other, the inessential, the object."[17] The contrasts of different forms of duality within the social arena point to a deeper opposition: a "fundamental hostility toward every other consciousness." The Husser-lian/Sartrean notion of consciousness as intentionality, a neutral zone, is not exactly ignored, but paired with the Hegelian notion that conscious-ness operates within a contest between two poles, where each pole is a combatant across a battlefield. Yet in woman's case, the battle has been lost; what remains is an oppressive situation, for "woman . . . nevertheless finds herself living in a world where men compel her to assume the status of the Other."[18] This analysis is close to Sartre's discussion of relations with others in *Being and Nothingness*; he defines relations with others as strongly conflictual, along the lines of Hegel's master-slave dialectic, which the French existentialists so appreciated. But Beauvoir insists that the dialectic doesn't "move" between women and men. To make her revolutionary argument here, she employs Hegelian premises (now suspect to feminist philosophy): first, it is due to the "imperialism of human consciousness" that a "one," a subject, becomes Other. Such a claim of a "universal" to human consciousness, and especially the strongly-worded description of this phenomenon that she provides, cannot be deduced from phenomenological notions like Heidegger's *Mitsein*. "No," she states, "this phenomenon is a result of the imperialism of the human consciousness, seeking always to exercise its sovereignty in objective fashion. . . . Human consciousness . . . included the original category of the Other and an original aspiration to dominate the Other."[19] Thus the oppression of woman is due to the characteristic nature of consciousness, and its impulse to "other-ize" another consciousness. Never could woman's physical weakness nor, indeed, any empirical fact be reason enough for such oppression. What stands behind empirical, historical oppression is the very nature of consciousness, which is conflictual.

Hegel's notion of consciousness underwent a remarkable change, as Beauvoir created her own theory. The Hegelian dialectic, with its opposing poles of subject-object, helped her describe the objectification of woman into a non-self, a nonessential being. But while Hegel's notion of the subject-object dialectic permitted the subject and object status to move from one person to another, in Beauvoir's analysis, in male-female relations, this dialectical movement freezes. This means that conscious-ness itself is gendered as a result of patriarchal relations. Normally two consciousnesses achieve reciprocal and competing claims of authority, but here there is no "reciprocity . . . recognized between the sexes," and "one of the contrasting terms is set up as the sole essential, denying any relativity in regard to its correlative and defining the latter as pure otherness"; the political consequence of this ontological fact is that "women do not dispute male sovereignty."[20] Beauvoir was claiming here that, at least up to the time of the writing of this book, movement toward the status of subject was not possible for woman, due to the lack of reciprocity between the sexes which defined who could (and could not) claim and achieve authority.

Locking into immobility what should be the reciprocal movement of the dialectic, according to Beauvoir's analysis, is the *unmoving* structure of patriarchy, a foundation whereby males hold all of the significant power—familial, religious, and political, and whereby the subject-self, if female, is a nonsubject, a secondary, relative being, an *Other*. By so stressing the otherness of woman in *The Second Sex*, Beauvoir qualifies both the existentialist perspective of subjectivity and the Hegelian perspective of reciprocity. No longer a "freedom," the for-itself as woman is Other, absolute Other, and thus never for-itself. The simplicity of the distinction between the for-itself and the in-itself from *The Ethics of Ambiguity* has now been greatly complicated. In *The Second Sex*, Beauvoir departs from Sartrean existentialism; with the help of Hegel and Levi-Strauss, she uncovers a plot in all history, one could say, to objectify a for-itself—woman.

The notion of the self developed in the Introduction to *The Second Sex* follows closely in many respects to that in her earlier work, *The Ethics of Ambiguity*. The for-itself is a free, surpassing, transcendent being, a subjectivity which exists through projects and which is distinguished from being-in-itself. This being-for-itself is an individual, and as such is sovereign, autonomous, and unique. One of the strongest declarations of this position comes at the end of the Introduction where Beauvoir announces that the standpoint from which she makes her analysis is existentialist ethics, a philosophical position which asserts that the actions and projects of the individual are the realization of transcendence and, therefore, of human freedom.[21] But there are important additions in *The Second Sex* to the existentialist notion of the self advanced in *The Ethics of Ambiguity*. Woman, being human, is a subject; she is being-for-itself. Thus, she is a sovereign, a unique individual, carrying the "essential" quality that all subjectivity carries, yet "the drama of woman lies in this conflict between the fundamental aspirations of every subject . . . who always regards the self as the essential—and the compulsions of a situation in which she is the inessential."[22] Woman's being is freedom in the mode of negativity, in the mode of transcending, but woman's situation makes her "inessential." What this amounts to is that the for-itself is differentiated according to gender, since "men compel [woman] to assume the status of the Other. . . . They propose to stabilize her as object and to doom her to immanence."[23] The freedom of the for-itself has been arbitrarily abridged, and facticity has been encouraged by (to use the language of *Ethics*) "parties of oppression" who maintain individuals of the female gender in a perpetual situation of oppression. Woman, being human, is a subject, that is, a free and autonomous existent with the ability to make choices. Yet, this transcendence in woman is burdened with a situation which requires her to be a nonsubject, a nonautonomous existent. Compelled into immanence by men, treated as an object, in fact, forced to live out the status of Other to consciousness, women are ontologically trapped, unable to live fulfilling lives.[24] The female for-itself, forced to be nonintentional being, an in-itself, is a nonsubject, in that she has been automatically and perpetually demeaned to the status of an in-itself—"immanence, stagnation . . . a degradation of existence into the *'en-soi'*—the brutish life of subjection to given conditions—and of liberty into constraint and contingence."[25] This equation of maleness with transcendence and femaleness with immanence is one that runs through-out the history of patriarchy, and women are caught in this situation of oppression.

In *The Ethics of Ambiguity*, Beauvoir had established that oppression is the denial of freedom, and freedom is the being of the for-itself; therefore, oppression is the denial of one's being. Thus, the female for-itself can't transcend, due *not* to an *internal* problem, for example, bad faith—Sartre's famous case—but to *external* conditions. This leads her to ask, "How can independence be recovered in a state of dependence? What circum-stances limit woman's liberty and how can they be overcome?"[26] These circumstances, the result of the fact that man has compelled woman to be the Other, that man has "won from the start," [27] have combined to create the denial of transcendence, a degradation of existence, which she calls "an absolute evil."[28] Such an evil, Beauvoir claims, is either a moral fault, if the subject consents, or an oppression, if the subject is constrained by others. Women will be doomed to immorality unless they free themselves as, "endeavoring to make their escape from the sphere hitherto assigned them, they aspire to full membership in the human race," in spite of the difficulties.[29]

The constraint that woman suffers due to social, cultural oppression is a denial of choice, since it is through one's own projects that the self transcends itself. To be woman is to be Other, but it is also still to be subject, even given the subjection under which this particular subjectivity usually functions, for this oppression can never be complete enough to make the for-itself nothing but immanence.[30] The result is immanence rather than transcendence, the being of the *en-soi*, not the *pour-soi*. Such is woman's "drama," her conflict. And if she manages to overcome external male-imposed constraints, she is caught in internal conflict, because insofar as she succeeds, she defeats her *feminine* self, as a subject-self, since "there is a contradiction between her status as a real human being and her vocation as a female."[31] An autonomous existence for woman conflicts with woman's self as the Other, for to be feminine is to be nonautonomous, passive, and "she must try to please . . . make herself object . . . thus a vicious circle is formed."[32] This conflict is incarnated in the body, since within the existential-phenomenological perspective of *The Second Sex*, the body—which the subject *is*—is not a thing. Its existence is never merely factual: "it is a situation, as viewed . . . [by] Heidegger, Sartre, and Merleau-Ponty: it is the instrument of our grasp upon the world."[33]

Directly related to the for-itself's existence-as-body is the body as sexual, erotic existence. But the contradiction which meets a female self (in that her success as self means the realization of transcendence, but - also her failure as a female [other/object]), also meets the female self in sexual experience. According to Beauvoir, erotic experience itself intensely reveals the ambiguity of the for-itself, both as subject and object for another. But the female self begins by experiencing itself as object. Here, the woman's status as subject is twice in question in sexuality; "at first she feels herself to be object and does not at once realize a sure independence in sex enjoyment. . . . Whether she adjusts herself more or less exactly to her passive role, woman is always frustrated as an active individual," says Beauvoir.[34]

Taking account of *The Second Sex* from one perspective, that of existentialist philosophy, one might say that Beauvoir's notion of the self becomes flawed philosophically because of the emphasis she places upon woman's "situation" in this work. Reflecting on those twin existentialist notions which are so fundamental to Sartrean philosophy—freedom and facticity—one can say that whereas the existentialist philosophy in *The Ethics of Ambiguity* stressed the use of one's freedom and the respect of the freedom of others as the core of morality, the philosophy of *The Second Sex* stresses facticity and shows that, in the historical, sociological, and cultural long view (avoided by traditional existentialism, with its stress on the individual subject), the "situation" of a certain group, for example, women, is so impressed upon the individual as to hamper or prevent the use of freedom—the individual's transcendence of their facticity. To say as she does in the Introduction to Book Two of *The Second Sex* that she will "describe the *common* basis that underlies every individual feminine existence" (italics added) is to radically undercut the notion of freedom relative to "every individual feminine existence," since through that common basis woman is "confined."[35]   It is also to radically change the focus of the analysis of human existence that existentialist philosophy had made from Kierkegaard to Sartre.

So, although she began her study from the philosophical standpoint of early Sartrean existentialism with its claim of radical freedom, Beauvoir nevertheless chose to maintain, in the Introduction to *The Second Sex*, that the reason women do not assert themselves as subjects is their situation: "women lack concrete means for organizing themselves into a unit which can stand face to face with the correlative unit," she says.[36]   Continuing this with an analysis that insists on the enforced condition of immanence, or facticity, to women by "man the subject," Beauvoir claims that such conditions exist, and that they are part of a situation of coercion which is external to women's own choices.   This situation is accomplished by what she called "the parties of oppression" in *Ethics*.   Thus, she shifts the analysis of existentialist ethics away from the freedom of the for-itself (in this case, the subjectivity of the female), toward facticity, in particular the facticity created by the oppression of a whole gender, in order "to describe the common basis that underlies every individual feminine existence."[37]   Beauvoir is always careful to maintain that she is not a determinist.   We may, however, conclude that, in describing woman's situation, she de-emphasizes the individual's freedom for the group's limits, moving very close to determinism indeed.[38]   While Sartre had emphasized, in his analysis of the facticity of the for-itself, that it was always accompanied by freedom, Beauvoir emphasized that for women the freedom was always accompanied by facticity, because the patriarchal system encouraged women's immanence and discouraged their transcendence.   Such a change in emphasis in Sartrean existentialism was one that Sartre also made, but only several years later, when he wrote *Saint Genet*.

A general analysis of the commonalities of any *group* of individual existents does not make the use of existentialist categories impossible by any means, though it does change the emphasis of the analysis.   Each individual human being experiences facticity, according to Sartre in *Being and Nothingness*, whether or not one calls this being "confined."   The innovation represented by *The Second Sex* is twofold: not only is the emphasis of its analysis on facticity rather than freedom, but individual facticity does not remain individual; it is generalized—genderized—since Beauvoir describes the common basis of the lives of all women, a basis provided by education and custom.

To what extent was this gendered self a departure from orthodox existentialism?   When approached as history of ideas, *The Second Sex* is a highly complex work. Though the basic prescription in *The Second Sex* for the "sickness" of the patriarchal era's creation of the otherness and immanence of woman is existentialist, since a cure must be given to individual patients, the sickness itself is cultural. The "woman" of *The Second Sex*, the Other to man, is a cultural object, not an individual. Beauvoir's analysis might be called a phenomenological description of "woman," though not of a particular woman nor of women. Whenever the discussion calls upon the lives of actual women, as it does in Book Two's series of chapters ("the child," "the independent woman," "the mystic," etc.), and when she uses the experiences of actual women from their writing, or even from research on women, as in psychoanalytic studies, she is careful to discuss the problems of their lives, the suffering of these "for-itselves" forced into the "brutish life of subjection to given conditions."[39]

No other existentialist had written on a cultural object, that is, taken on the task of a description of a socially constructed entity. Existentialism was profoundly interested in the assertion of freedom, but profoundly disinterested in producing, in its *theoretical* works, concrete examinations of freedom (or its denial by external oppression or internal dishonesty). The attraction of novels and plays, particularly for the French existentialists, was that such genres provided ways to show how (fictional) people lived out their freedom. Sartre came closest to the elaboration of a cultural object in *Anti-Semite and Jew*, published in 1946. But that work is vastly different; its differences from *The Second Sex* are instructive. Sartre's analysis is a discussion of the personality of the oppressor, of the mind of the anti-Semite: "anti-Semitism is more than a mere 'opinion' about the Jews . . . it involves the entire personality of the anti-Semite. . . . he has a method of thought and a conception of the world all his own. In fact, we cannot state what he affirms without implicit reference to certain intellectual principles."[40] But Sartre's study follows the "method of thought and conception of the world" of the anti-Semite, his/her "intellect." Sartre's analysis itself of this intellect really remains on the speculative level. When he discusses the Jew (a discussion that can be seen as analogous to Beauvoir's description of woman), he acknowledges the importance of *situation*, as Beauvoir does for woman, but Sartre never concretizes his analysis as Beauvoir did; he alludes to the facticity of the Jew, but never discusses it with any significant detail. He begins with a point of existentialist principle: "If it is agreed that man may be defined as a being having freedom within the limits of a situation, then it is easy to see that the exercise of this freedom may be considered as *authentic* or *inauthentic*," he says.[41] But his analysis fastens on the *mind* of either the anti-Semite or the Jew, rather than the situation which has been created and in which both live. When he does discuss the issue of situation, it is always within the context of the internal rather than external structure of that situation; "the situation which [the Jew] has to lay claim to and to live in is quite simply that of a martyr."[42] The Jew's situation is present in a general way:

What the least favored of men ordinarily discover in their *situation* is a bond of concrete solidarity with other men. . . . But we have shown that the Jews have neither community of interests nor community of beliefs. They do not have the same fatherland; they have no history. The sole tie that binds them is the hostility and disdain of the societies which surround them. . . . The *situation* he wishes fully to understand and live out is . . . almost incomprehensible: it is an atmosphere.[43] [italics added]

Though Sartre's book acknowledges situation (the aspect of "facticity" in the existentialist notion of the self), it never paints a picture of that situation. It provides an outline for an analysis of an oppressed group, but that analysis remained abstract. The similarities to this passage in one of Beauvoir's from the Introduction are striking. According to Sartre and Beauvoir respectively, neither Jews nor women have a history, nor any basis for solidarity. Both live dispersed among the oppressing class (surely there were many Jews living in ghettoes in Europe, but not all Jews were ghetto Jews). Beauvoir says, in one of her most famous passages from *The Second Sex*:

women . . . have no past, no history, no religion of their own; and they have no such solidarity of work and interest as that of the proletariat. They are not even promiscuously herded together in the way that creates community feeling among the American Negroes, the ghetto Jews. . . . They live dispersed among the males . . . they feel solidarity with men of [their] class, not with . . . women.[44]

In contrast to Sartre's study of the mind of the anti-Semite, Beauvoir's study of woman's situation ran to nearly a thousand pages of detail in which she created a portrait of the cultural object, "woman," including research on everything from biology and psychology, to the history of women in antiquity and modernity, and the experiences of women as wives, mothers, writers, gleaned from their writings. Her study took her far afield from the existentialist formulas of the for-itself. It took her into an interpretation of "woman," an object structured by specific institutions, specific holy writings, specific sufferings, and into the creation of a detailed picture of a system, the patriarchal oppression of women.

Thus, Michèle LeDoeuff is only partly correct; *The Second Sex* is not deterministic. However, it *is* an empirical study, informed with the philosophical foundation of existential phenomenology, steeped heavily in early Hegel and helped by the new type of analysis (structuralism) that her colleague Levi-Strauss was creating.[45] Uniquely non-existentialist about Beauvoir's analysis of woman is her method of providing a good deal of verification for the theoretical framework she sets down in the Introduction.[46]

We know that the starting point of Beauvoir's writing of *The Second Sex* was her decision to write about her own life. With that personal standpoint, the formulas of existentialism may have looked inadequate indeed. Her first step for *The Second Sex* was research. Such a choice was an acknowledgment of her commitment to the "facts" of facticity, beyond the general assertion of the existence of facticity in the for-itself, as much if not more than to the more expected existentialist stress on the freedom of the for-itself. An empirical study steeped in Hegelian-existentialist-phenomenological-structuralist theory, *The Second Sex* was written because Beauvoir chose to tell her own life story. In this work, she progressed from heroic assertions of freedom and vague acknowledgments of facticity to the actual details from which freedom and facticity are present for a whole gender. Thus she could progress to the study of facticity and freedom as they were embodied in one human life: "I was born at four o'clock in the morning on the 9th of January 1908 in a room fitted with white-enamelled furniture and overlooking the boulevard Raspail," she matter-of-factly begins.[47]

NOTES

1. Simone de Beauvoir, *Force of Circumstance*, trans. Richard Howard (New York: Harper Colophon Books, 1977), p. 94. (Hereafter, *Force.*)

2. *Force*, pp. 94–5.

3. For Beauvoir's discussion of the reaction to this work, see *Force*, pp. 185–93. One should remember that she not only wrote *The Second Sex* before the current women's movement (it was published in 1949), but she explained the circumstances of its writing, evaluated it, and discussed its reception before the women's movement also; that is, in 1963, with her third volume of autobiography, *Force of Circumstance*. In her acutely perceptive evaluation, she apologized for the book's style and composition, said that she was discovering her ideas as she was explaining them, and admitted that her writing was a bit inelegant and repetitious. But she never disavowed its ideas. Thirty years later, discussing it in an interview with Alice Schwarzer, she was still reeling a bit from the book's reception. See Alice Schwarzer, *After "The Second Sex": Conversations wiith Simone de Beauvoir*, trans. Marianne Howarth (New York: Pantheon Books, 1984), pp. 41–3.

4. Simone de Beauvoir, *The Second Sex*, trans. H. M. Parshley (New York: Vintage, 1989), p. xix.

5. See Introduction, first endnote, for explanation of my spelling of Other.

6. *The Second Sex*, p. xxx.

7. *The Second Sex*, p. xix. Beauvoir doesn't identify this quotation, but it is likely that she had in mind Thomas Aquinas.

8. *The Second Sex*, p. xx.

9. *The Second Sex*, "Introduction to Book Two"; this is unnumbered in the Vintage edition, but follows p. xxxvi.

10. *The Second Sex*, pp. xx–xxi.

11. *The Second Sex*, p. xx.

12. *The Second Sex*, p. xxii.

13. *The Second Sex*, p. xxxv. Here, Beauvoir never used the word "ego" in the French. This was simply an addition of the translator. She used "*sujet*"; the word "*sujet*" clearly connects the sentence to the rest of the existentialist theory in the passage, whereas the word "ego" is misleading, particularly for an English-speaking audience, which would tend to connect it to Freudian notions of the psyche.

14. Michèle LeDoeuff, "Simone de Beauvoir and Existentialism," *Feminist Studies* 6 (1980), pp. 277–89. This article is frequently quoted in scholarship on *The Second Sex*.

15. This essay has been traditionally known as "Existentialism Is a Humanism," but recently it was titled, "The Humanism of Existentialism" in Jean-Paul Sartre, *Essays in Existentialism*, ed. Wade Baskin (Secaucus, NJ: Citadel Press, 1974), p. 41.

16. LeDoeuff, p. 286.

17. *The Second Sex*, p. xxiii.

18. *The Second Sex*, p. xxxv. Beauvoir's interest in Hegel's problem stems at least from her first published work, *She Came to Stay*, published in French in 1943. The epigraph is a quote from Hegel: "Each consciousness seeks the death of the other."

19. *The Second Sex*, pp. 57–8.

20. *The Second Sex*, p. xxiv.

21. *The Second Sex*, p. xxxiv.

22. *The Second Sex*, p. xxxv.

23. *The Second Sex*, p. xxxv. Here the translator has decided to translate a specifically phenomenological term, *conscience*, consciousness, for the psychoanalytically-loaded term, "ego." Compare this with the next line of the Introduction where he decided to translate *sujet* as "subject," but to add in parentheses "ego": "the drama of woman lies in this conflict between the fundamental aspirations of every subject (ego)—who always regards the self as the essential—and the compulsions of a situation in which she is the inessential." (In the French original, "regards the self" is the reflexive, "*se pose*.")

24. *The Second Sex*, p. xxxv.

25. *The Second Sex*, p. xxxiii.

26. *The Second Sex*, p. xxxv.

27. *The Second Sex*, p. xxvii.

28. *The Second Sex*, p. xxxv.

29. *The Second Sex*, p. xxxv. Beauvoir had said *"mitsein humain,"* rather than "membership in the human race," having used *"mitsein"* earlier (p. xxiii). See also Mary Wollstonecraft, *Vindication of the Rights of Woman*, ed. C. Hagelman, Jr. (New York: W. W. Norton, 1967), chapter 2, passim. Wollstonecraft makes a similar argument. She claims that since there is a strong connection between morality and the use of reason, the blame that belongs to men for not allowing women the use of their reason also extends to women's immorality. Some scholars identify Beauvoir and Wollstonecraft as "rationalist feminists," for this reason.

30. *The Second Sex*, p. 51. Beauvoir writes, "the Other nevertheless remains subject in the midst of her resignation."

31. *The Second Sex*, p. 336.

32. *The Second Sex*, p. 280.

33. *The Second Sex*, p. 34.

34. *The Second Sex*, pp. 402–3.

35. *The Second Sex*, p. xxxvi.

36. *The Second Sex*, p. xxv.

37. *The Second Sex*, p. xxxvi. The term "basis" is a translation for the French *"fond,"* which may be translated as "essence." In that case, the sentence would read: "to describe the common essence that underlies every individual feminine existence." If one were to use that translation, it would indicate a deliberate and interesting twist to Sartrean existentialism's motto, since it would be asserting that "essence is prior to existence," rather than "existence is prior to esence."

38. *The Second Sex*, p. xxxv.

39. *The Second Sex*, p. xxxv.

40. Jean-Paul Sartre, *Anti-Semite and Jew*, trans. George J. Becker (New York: Grove Press, 1962), p. 33 (originally published in French as *Réflexions sur la Question Juive*, 1946).

41. Sartre, *Anti-Semite*, p. 90.

42. Sartre, *Anti-Semite*, p. 91.

43. Sartre, *Anti-Semite*, p. 91.

44. *The Second Sex*, p. xxv.

45. See her footnote about that on p. xxiii of *The Second Sex*.

46. In fact, she tells us in her autobiography that she began the project with library research; we are to assume that the theoretical framework she crafted in the Introduction grew out of her empirical research. See *Force*, p. 94.

47. Simone de Beauvoir, *Memoirs of a Dutiful Daughter*, trans. James Kirkup (New York: Harper Colophon Books, 1974), p. 5. Original French publication, 1958; English translation, 1959.

3

Techniques for Writing the Self

It is clear that Beauvoir went beyond Sartrean philosophy, particularly in *The Ethics of Ambiguity* and *The Second Sex*. But she used more than these works alone to express the complexity and depth of her thinking on the self; as did most of the other French existentialists, she used a variety of literary genres to convey her philosophical analyses. Yet it was from the standpoint of autobiographer that she would create her most profound analysis of the self. The theory and practice of this autobiographical writing, as well as some of its techniques and structures, bear studying.

Beauvoir's creation of the notion of the gendered self in *The Second Sex* is a radical departure from the theory of the existential self already in place in *The Ethics of Ambiguity* and a variety of other essays. In a number of passages within the autobiographies, Beauvoir presents some particular manifestations of these two notions of the self within her own self-life-story, and at times engages in direct discussions of the self. I first examine these introspective passages—the places in the text where the autobiographer stops the narrative and questions or comments upon it. After this, I examine places within the narrative where, by retrospection, the narrator displays the existential and gendered self.[1] In the retrospective passages, I identify three faces, selves, personas, that Beauvoir crafted for us in her autobiographies: the child, the woman in love, and the writer.

TWO SELVES

In the formal philosophical terms she might have used, Beauvoir would say that her autobiographical project was a meaning-giving action, the work of a consciousness in a present reflecting on its past, creating a past "self," and in some places projecting a future "self." In existential-phenomenological terms, this reflection is a creation of a "self" in the substantial sense of self, a giving-meaning to consciousness which, without reflection, remains empty and "unselfed," since the existential self, the for-itself, is a nothingness. Thus, the creation of this "self" through the memoirs is the creation of a "self" that is not the self of consciousness. In existentialist terms, the narrator is filling the self, or making it an in-itself, giving it the being of things; "the self-knowing act is a self-negating act," Hugh Silverman has written.[2]   This existentialist-phenomenological notion of the self, inherited from Hegel and Husserl through Sartre and Heidegger and used in *The Ethics of Ambiguity*, is that of a for-itself which is free, has projects, is a nothingness, and performs as a subjectivity by making choices. This was directly discussed by Beauvoir and had obvious philosophical credentials. But, as we have seen, there is a second notion of the self at work in her writings: the gendered self, the product of her own analysis of woman in *The Second Sex*. It was never acknowledged as the existential self was, nor did it have any philosophical ancestry. Beauvoir had taken part in creating and defending the existential self, as Sartre's major reader and as writer of *The Ethics of Ambiguity*, as well as other essays and novels. The second, the gendered self, she created in *The Second Sex*.

Beauvoir used both notions of the self, the existential self and the gendered self, when she wrote her autobiographies. Written over a period of sixteen years, her autobiography is a very large body of work, nearly twenty-two hundred pages in the original French. (One scholar suggests that this may be one of the longest autobiographies in any language by a woman.)[3] It includes the four volumes I will discuss: *Memoirs of a Dutiful Daughter*, *The Prime of Life*, *Force of Circumstance*, and *All Said and Done*. Other works, such as *A Very Easy Death* and *Adieux: A Farewell to Sartre*, could be added to the list, since the first is a narration of the events leading up to her mother's death from cancer, and the second (published in 1981) includes a year-by-year narration of Sartre's last ten years, until his death in 1980.[4] But, under another principle of classification, a serious enough issue in the genre of autobiography, the autobiographical works might also include reports of her travels, such as *The Long March* and *America Day by Day*. Indeed it could include, under still another principle of classification, the novels *She Came to Stay*, *The Blood of Others*, and especially *The Mandarins*.[5]

DEFINING AUTOBIOGRAPHY

A listing of Beauvoir's works which appears at the front of *Adieux* (the last work she published) shows that by the principles of classification of an unknown editor at Gallimard, *A Very Easy Death* is listed as "*un récit*" (a report, a narrative account). The other works I have chosen to call autobiography are listed in the category, "*Essais–Littérature*," which includes *The Second Sex* and *The Coming of Age*, as well as works most scholars would unquestioningly term "philosophy": *The Ethics of Ambiguity*, *Privilèges*, and the books on her travels to China and the United States. No category of "autobiography" is used at all in this listing.[6]

The tremendous amount of material presented in the four volumes of Beauvoir's autobiography makes generalizations not only difficult, but questionable. I will be claiming only that my own selection and highlighting of details, my own presentation of her presentations of a "self" in the autobiographies, is fair, not that it is exhaustive by any means. I have identified points of contact between her philosophical notions of the self and her own presentations of a "self," but this project does not address the issue of what other treasures may lie in the autobiographical presentation of a "self" by a highly intellectual autobiographer whose writings are numerous.

Formal structural elements, such as prefaces and epilogues, call the reader's attention to the distinction between introspection and retrospection. They provide the autobiographical narrator with direct and relatively easy occasions for introspection on the self. However, because they clearly mark boundaries within the text, they may serve to actually limit the introspective practice of the autobiographer (rather, the *autobiographer* may choose to limit introspection to these sections), so that it never overflows into the story/history of the "real" life, if the writer considers that to be the retrospective account of the self.

Relevant to the issue of introspection and retrospection in Beauvoir's autobiographical writings, a survey of her textual architecture reveals that in *Memoirs* there is no dedication, no preface, and no epilogue. The book is divided into four parts, with no chapters dividing the parts. *The Prime of Life* begins with a dedication to Jean-Paul Sartre and a prologue rendered as "preface" in the English version. This prologue refers the reader to her project, as discussed before. The book is divided into three parts and these are divided into chapters. There is no formal ending, yet the volume ends with a discussion of death, whereas the *Memoirs* had ended with an actual death—that of her friend, Zaza. Then follows a reflection on writing, including issues of literary honesty, authors, and the like, which directs the reader to the process of the writing of the text itself. This text, through the strategy of the prologue and also the dedication, as well as its more elaborate segmentation, calls greater attention to itself as a text and to its organization than does *Memoirs*. *Force of Circumstance* surprisingly carries no dedication, although after the greater structural sophistication of the second volume, one would expect this authorial tactic to be maintained. In other ways, its organization reflects a growth of structural complexity, for the book is divided into two parts (the English paperback is printed in two volumes) and it carries a prologue, although it is untitled; it also includes an "*intermède*" ("interlude" in English) and an epilogue. The final volume, *All Said and Done,* carries a dedication, "*A Sylvie*," to Sylvie Le Bon, the young woman who became a friend of Beauvoir's, and eventually her adopted daughter and executor of her estate. The text carries a prologue and is segmented into no large divisions, but into eight chapters. It has no epilogue, yet at the end Beauvoir calls our attention to the need for an ending. She calls upon her readers to supply a conclusion to this volume; hence, it ends with a call for an ending beyond the writing of the author herself.[7]

So Beauvoir's first autobiographical work, *Memoirs of a Dutiful Daughter,* begins with none of the formal introspective structures; in contrast, the last autobiographical work, *All Said and Done,* might be described as nothing but introspection. In *Memoirs* there are no introductory, middle, or concluding statements. Since the only introspection on the self occurs within her narrative account of the past, it is always (formally at least) about the moment or period being recalled and never straightforwardly, unambiguously, about the self. She does, however, provide summaries from time to time of her self during the stages of her life that she is recalling. (These generalizations about the self will be discussed later.) However, since they always function as the narrator's summaries of a Time Past and a Person Past, summaries of Person Present never appear. The other three volumes, in which she does offer summary statements about her self (Person Present), exhibit the opposite problem: the announced theory of the self that the reader meets is not necessarily what the protagonist, "Simone de Beauvoir," really used in living out her life, or even in deciding on how to write about it. But it is present there at least, offered by the author as the "real" understanding of the self, the real or correct notion of the "lived self." For this reason, I discuss it as though it were the "real" lived self, even though there is really no way to arrive at the "real" intentions or understanding of the self of the protagonist beyond what the author presents.

Only after *Memoirs of a Dutiful Daughter* did Beauvoir segment her works and provide introspective commentaries by means of prefaces, epilogues, and even mid-text reflective statements (sometimes titled, sometimes not). But though *Memoirs* had no formal preface, it had a preface, a monumental one—*The Second Sex.* Beauvoir explained, in *Force of Circumstance*, that *The Second Sex* was conceived more or less accidentally, preparatory to beginning her autobiography, since when she started her autobiography, she asked herself: "What has it meant to me to be a woman?"[8] Later in the same work, she recast this into a more directly philosophical project when she said she wanted to determine "the condition of woman in general."[9] This detour, begun in 1946 and lasting for two years, was followed by another writing project, and yet another during the writing of *The Second Sex* itself, so that the autobiographical work was postponed for another ten years.[10] The project was conceived at first as a single, self-contained work, with no intention by Beauvoir to develop it further. But the ending statement of *Memoirs* drew her further on, into the second volume, the third, and the fourth.

THE CHRONOLOGICAL ORDER

William Spengemann notes that there are different ways in which chronology may affect autobiography. The autobiographer chooses the pattern by which events and experiences are offered, taking a more or less chronologically oriented one, but within that choice, she or he may take a distinctly causal pattern or one focused around certain crucial events.[11] Beauvoir chose the latter course. This is also the one most suitable to an existentialist outlook, since a focus on key events stresses the importance of individual actions and reactions to external events, and emphasizes the importance of direct, individual responses to the contingencies the world continually provides.

In all but the last of her autobiographies, Beauvoir followed a roughly chronologized scheme organized around certain crucial events. In *Memoirs*, those events were the meeting of Beauvoir and Sartre and the death of Zaza. In *The Prime of Life*, crucial events included the publication of her first works; the "ménage à trois" of Simone, Olga, and Sartre; and World War II. In *Force of Circumstance*, most significant were: her travels, the affairs with Algren and Lanzmann; the Algerian War; and the political activities of the French Left, including the founding of the journal *LTM* (*Les Temps Modernes*). By contrast, *All Said and Done* is organized thematically, as I noted earlier. Yet it stands as the distillation of the other works, since instead of focusing only on major events, it uses a combination of these (e.g., the founding of the American and French women's movements) and other important themes that are distilled from them: writing and traveling, most notably.

But the chronological structure of her autobiographical work is not easily detected. Though she followed a roughly chronologized schema, she seldom dated events for her readers. In this way she undercut, if not excluded, the importance of "clock time," the positivity of temporality. In any case, chronology is not primary in her autobiographies; what is primary is the continual philosophization of her life experience: her writing, her relationships—with Sartre and others—and the importance of "History" in her life.

Philippe Lejeune, a noted French theorist of autobiography, criticizes Beauvoir's autobiography on two counts: first, her use of the chronological order; second, her use of a notion of the past which, as a good Sartrean, she should have rejected, that is, the "past-in-itself."[12] Though the details of this notion had not been worked out by Sartre, in Lejeune's opinion this was no excuse for Beauvoir's use of a "past-in-itself." Sartre had written an autobiography, *The Words*, which at least creatively avoided those pitfalls to which Beauvoir's autobiography succumbed, says Lejeune. So, though Sartre had not put an adequate positive theory in place to direct a good Sartrean existentialist in a retelling of the past, he had taken two important steps: first, he had conceived a theory of what the past was *not*, that is, it did not have an immanence, in other words, there was no "being-in-itself" of the past, no "past-in-itself"; and second, he had shown, by his own practice—the writing of *The Words*—an innovative strategy for a retrospective story of a life, his own.[13]

Lejeune's critique of Beauvoir's autobiography begins with an obvious point about Sartre: that in his existential philosophy, specifically in *Being and Nothingness*, Sartre created a notion of temporality fitting his notion of the human being—one which asserts that the self, the for-itself, is a nothingness, a freedom which exists as a surpassing, or transcendence.

In his novels, Sartre was able to stress, in fact focus on, the freedom of the for-itself. When the writer's temporal perspective changes however, when one looks back at other lives as well as one's own (as Sartre did with the series of biographies he wrote—of Baudelaire, Flaubert, and Genet), as well as with his own autobiography, the realm of freedom may seem to be more burdened by facticity. The character whose life the writer describes will become an object studied. Lejeune contends that a Sartrean account of existence seems to function on two very different orders: that of fiction, focused on the present and emphasizing freedom; and that of biography, focused on the past and emphasizing determinism.[14]

Beauvoir's use of the chronological order in her autobiographies raises ontological problems, Lejeune notes, since when an author employs the chronological order to tell her story, she reflects by that use a naive and positivist view of "the way things are"; she accepts the traditional view of history, including her own history, as linear. A specific and objectified conception of the human being accompanies this notion of time, and it is this conception of the human being that is unsuitable to Sartrean existentialism. As a good Sartrean, Beauvoir should have avoided this pitfall, Lejeune feels.[15]

In the prologue to *All Said and Done,* Beauvoir did choose another approach, a thematic one. This example of her divergence from the chronological order hardly satisfied Lejeune, however. He criticized it as too easy a solution; the thematic "order" she used in this work was "in reality not an order but a form of accounting," he said.[16] Beauvoir provides us with an explanation of her selection of a thematic order in the work, and in so doing, explains her reasons for using the chronological order elsewhere: "a chronological sequence . . . has its drawbacks . . . my [earlier] account turns my history into a finite reality: and it is not a finite reality. . . . By following the sequence of time, I put it out of my power to convey . . . interconnections."[17] Properly self-critical from a Sartrean philosophical standpoint, Beauvoir maintains that, even so, this was the only route open to her: "For me life was an undertaking that had a clear direction, and in giving an account of mine I had to follow its progress."[18] While Beauvoir asserts her belief in the Sartrean notion of a life "project" in this statement, indirectly, she also expresses ambivalence to Sartrean philosophy. Earlier, I noted her differences with Sartrean philosophy by her development of what I called "the gendered self." But central to the existential notion of the self is the claim that it is a subject with control over its own life, that by making the most important choices in it, it creates over time, an "essence." This is Sartre's well-known "existence precedes essence" claim.

Lejeune's criticism of Beauvoir for her use of a "past-in-itself" is important in pointing out her divergence from Sartrean philosophy. He is right in maintaining that she did not carry out the Sartrean "line" in her autobiographies, but wrong in assuming that she should have, or that it would have been fitting for her, as a writer, to do so. In relation to the development of her own thinking, Beauvoir's autobiography uses a proper methodology, one proper to *her*, for she created an autobiography that was at home with contradiction, in the same way *The Second Sex* was.

Beauvoir took great pride in being a writer, not a "philosopher," if by that is meant a systematizer. Her dislike of systematization would have led her to ignore those stipulations of the Sartrean system that Lejeune invokes:

it would be more useful to explain *how* certain individuals are capable of getting results from that conscious venture into lunacy known as a "philosophical system," from which they derive that obsessional attitude which endows their tentative patterns with universal insight and applicability. As I have remarked before, women are not by nature prone to obsessions of this type.[19]

Women *are* prone, however, to writing their memoirs. When Beauvoir wrote hers, she endowed them with philosophical concerns, even terminology, but not with the "lunacy" of a philosophical system.

AUTOBIOGRAPHICAL INTENTIONS

Though she offers no explanation in *Memoirs* of why she undertook its writing, in the preface to the second volume, *The Prime of Life*, she does explain why she wrote both the first volume and the second. The first volume she described as the story of a person who might soon disappear, one who had escaped her fate to win her freedom. "I had long wanted to set down the story of my first twenty years," she asserts; "Nothing, I feared, would survive of that girl, not so much as a pinch of ashes. . . . I took that child and that adolescent girl . . . [and] gave them a new existence—in black and white, on sheets of paper."[20]

Memoirs had ended with the event of the death and wake of her close friend, Zaza, who had struggled with her bourgeois family over her choice of a fiancé. The book ends in the following way: "She [Zaza] had often appeared to me at night, her face all yellow under a pink sun-bonnet, and seeming to gaze reproachfully at me. We had fought together against the revolting fate that had lain ahead of us, and for a long time I believed that I had paid for my own freedom with her death."[21] In the preface to *The Prime of Life* Beauvoir noted her reasons for writing *Memoirs*: "Some critics supposed that I meant *Memoirs of a Dutiful Daughter* as an object lesson for young girls; my main desire was to discharge a debt," she says.[22] Though Beauvoir never directly states what that debt was and to whom it was owed, the reader would probably be correct to assume that the debt was to Zaza. We can also assume that *Memoirs* was written to rid her of the ghost of Zaza, through "bearing witness" to the battle that they had fought together against family and bourgeois conformities. Indeed, in *Force of Circumstance*, she states that through this writing Zaza's ghost was exorcised; "Never again did she come back to see me in my dreams. Generally speaking, since it has been published and read, the story of my childhood and youth has detached itself from me entirely," she remarks.[23] So if the writing of *Memoirs* had been "to discharge a debt" to Zaza, it was first to discharge a debt to herself, as we have seen—to her adolescent self, to preserve it from disappearance into the fifty-year-old woman; and second, to rid herself of the ghost which pursued her.

She remarks later that she had not meant to continue this original project of the writing of her autobiography; in fact, at several places in the next volume, *Force of Circumstance*, narrating the story of those years in which she wrote the *Memoirs* and *The Prime of Life*, the late fifties, she makes it clear that she vacillated for a good while, asking advice from Sartre and other friends before deciding to continue with it.[24]

However, she did decide to continue, and in the preface to *The Prime of Life* she explains why: it was to narrate how she had used that freedom she had won from her family and class, in particular how her choice to be a writer had been realized. The profession of writing, which she had chosen and for which she had won her freedom from that bourgeois upbringing, might be described also; it was the very reason for the battle. So behind the last line of *Memoirs* was a question: how had she used her freedom, the freedom she had won, the freedom for which (supposedly) Zaza had died? Beauvoir wonders plaintively, "Freedom I had—but freedom to do what? . . . I had chosen to be a writer. . . . But *why*? . . . Little by little I became convinced that . . . the first volume of my *Memoirs* required a sequel."[25]

The third volume, perhaps motivated by her growing awareness of her own aging and mortality, was written to keep herself "alive." Beauvoir's intention to write a living narrative was intense at this point: "I wanted my blood to circulate in this narrative; I wanted to fling myself into it, still very much alive—to put myself in question before all questions are silenced. Perhaps it is too soon; but tomorrow it certainly will be too late."[26] Her sentiment here is reminiscent of one of the intentions in writing *Memoirs*, to "save" her past self from disappearance. Opening with the statement that she had stopped her autobiographical writing after *The Prime of Life* to test for more interest from her readers, Beauvoir uses the tactic of direct quotations ("Friends, readers, urged me on: 'And then? What happened next? . . . you owe us the rest'") to note that there *was* interest. Yet there were some others who made criticisms, and others who suggested she refrain from telling more, since her life had been public property, so to speak, since 1944.[27] To these she also gives a direct voice. It is, finally, to clear up the misunderstandings resulting from her celebrity status that she decided to continue, as well as to relate, in much greater detail than before, certain historical political events.

By the time she wrote the interlude in *Force of Circumstance,* she felt that she was falling into a trap (to her mind an innate defect of all autobiographers), namely that "'What goes without saying' goes without being said, and thus one misses the essential."[28] That unsaid essential turned out to be her work, her writing, the difficulty of which readers did not adequately appreciate, for to her it was "more than just a profession; it is a passion, or let us say, a madness."[29]

In *All Said and Done* she redefined her project, yet in a way that was in agreement with the thoughts presented in the interlude in *Force of Circumstance.* She took on the task of saying the as yet unsaid, those unsaid essentials, the important themes for which there had not been a place or time in her own autobiographical writing.[30] Her life was "an undertaking that had a clear direction," and her account of it paralleled its "progress," she says.[31] (The French is also written in this impersonal, passive tone, which asserts that the writer is following a task that must follow a direction: "*Il me fallait en suivre le cheminement.*")[32] This impersonality, amounting to an abrogation of responsibility, is clearest at the end of *All Said and Done,* when Beauvoir literally gives over to the reader the task of making a conclusion to her book—and so, to her life, perhaps.

In the prologue to *All Said and Done,* as she explains her reasons for writing this final volume, Beauvoir also addresses the question of methodology. She will *not* follow a chronological sequence here, but rather creates an organization by themes.[33] She also provides yet another explanation and defense of her continuance of her autobiography. It is specifically in order to relate her own old age to the issue of aging as presented in her book, *The Coming of Age,* that this last volume was written. This makes the autobiographical work a companion piece (in this case an epilogue) to a theoretical work, *The Coming of Age,* in the same way that *Memoirs* can be called a companion piece to its prologue, *The Second Sex.*

The four volumes of Beauvoir's autobiography differ considerably and in a variety of ways, aside from the most obvious one of material covered. It is important to note that when we relate the formal philosophy of Beauvoir to the autobiography, we are relating it not to the "literal" past self, that is, the child Simone, but to the narrator's description, selection, and judgment of the protagonist. Thus, the object of our analysis of the use of the philosophical "self" in the autobiography will be the narrator, not the subject of the autobiography. The subject, the past, historical Simone, like the content of a dream, is given only through the narration of the past (the dream as it is told). The child Simone is a phantom summoned up only through the voice of the narrator.

TONAL QUALITIES

The tone of *Memoirs* is often ironic, a feature more than one reader has commented on. The reader is made to understand that the narrator takes a certain distance from the protagonist; that distance is marked sometimes by amusement—an almost comedic detachment—even smug, sometimes, but in general a critical attitude.[34] Although humorous, the tone is a censuring one; it tells us that the narrator has judged the child and adolescent Simone for us. Even the book's title points to this ironic detachment: *Mémoires d'une jeune fille rangée*. The title of the work is an announcement of a genre; these are "memoirs," but they are impersonal; no name is given. This is not *The Autobiography of* (or *Memoirs of*) *Simone de Beauvoir*, but of "*une jeune fille*," a (young) girl. The English translator used the word "daughter," whereas a more literal translation of the French title would have been different in two ways, for it would have been *Memoirs of A Steady* (or *Ordered*, *Tidy*, or *Arranged*) *Young Girl*. The full play of the French word in the title, "*rangée*," is diminished in the English translation, which selects the word "dutiful"; "*rangée*" can mean "subdued" or "ordered," but also "ranked," and even "pitched," as in a "pitched battle," a meaning which would be suitable at many places in this text.

Through the linguistic strategy of a certain ironic detachment and not through any "announced" content, Beauvoir can be said to defend the existentialist notion that the self is no-thing, though the *reflected* self is some-thing, precisely a thing, since it resides outside the locus of the self (the for-itself, that is), outside of consciousness. Through her detached tone, Beauvoir informs us that this person, Simone, is part of the past, exists no longer, is not her self. Hence, the past self, the self as reflected (a substantial self, and not the "true" and immediate for-itself) is set off from the narrator, whose voice speaks in a kind of eternal present about the past. The tone helps to distance the narrator from the chronological order of the narrative as well.

Further, the tone functions as unannounced introspection, providing a commentary on the self that is more often than not self-deprecating. She repeatedly mocks her young self in relating stories of her family's and her own participation in the war effort (World War I) for France. Her father was called to active duty (though illness had resulted in his discharge earlier from the Reserve), and six-year-old Simone passionately embraced the cause, a dutiful daughter to her father and her nation-state:

I had already given proof of exemplary patriotism by stamping on a celluloid doll, "made in Germany," which belonged, by the way, to my sister. It was only with great difficulty that I was restrained from throwing out of the window our silver knife-rests, which were branded with the same infamous device. . . . "Simone is an ardent patriot," [the grown-ups] would say, with proud smiles. I stored the smiles away in my memory and developed a taste for unstinted praise.[35]

This passage mocks a number of things: Simone, the little girl who is the "great patriot"; patriotism itself; the grown-ups who admired such devotion to the cause; and finally, her strong dedication to her citizen/warrior/father, a failed lawyer and amateur actor who only in war had "let his moustache grow."[36] Like the man from the country in Kafka's "Before the Law," the young Simone was awed by this symbol of male power: "under his tarboosh [mustache] his face had a gravity which made a great impression on me."[37]

When she is relating the excesses of her late adolescence, in *Memoirs*, she tells one that concerns a visit from her cousin, Jacques, in whom she had an ongoing romantic interest for many years, and whom she nearly married. Beauvoir remembers the young Simone, who had begun the serious study of philosophy at the Institut Sainte-Marie, and how she was thrilled by a visit of Jacques to her and her parents. When she narrates the story for us, she includes a Cartesian echo: "That evening, as usual, he treated me like a little girl; but there was such kindness in his voice and in his smiles . . . When I laid my head on my pillow that night, my eyes filled with tears. 'I weep, therefore I love,' I told myself with rapturous melancholy. I was seventeen: it was the age for that sort of thing."[38] The longer she attended the Institut, the more resentful she became of her parents' conservatism (political, as well as personal) and their meddling in her affairs; she countered by rebelling in numerous ways. In describing Simone's reaction, Beauvoir moves quickly from a straightforward story of rebellion to an ironic description of a young woman who was full of social and moral pretensions. In one passage, she describes her intense admiration for a newfound hero, Robert Garric, a lecturer at the Institut, and an idealist and socialist reformer. She begins the passage in a standard narrative manner, saying "my parents did not find me to their liking, and so I deliberately made myself unpleasant," but by the end of the passage, she creates through parody an additional distance from this person who had rebelled against the adults.[39] Intent on escaping the pressures of the family, she promised herself that she would use Garric's example to transform her life: "I refused to be patient any longer; without further ado I set my feet upon the way to heroic heights."[40] Again, when discussing this stage in her life, Beauvoir mocks not the principles, but the motivations that were the foundations of her actions. She and her friends, young Parisian intellectuals of the 1920s, embraced "Disquiet," a sort of nihilism which sought to uncover the sham of traditional morality. But in her look back at the young, disquieted Simone, she is sarcastic:

I dedicated myself to the cult of Disquiet. . . . I lost no time in embracing the principles of immoralism. Of course, I did not approve of people stealing out of self-interest or going to bed with someone for the pure pleasure of it; but if these became quite gratuitous acts, acts of desperation and revolt—and, of course, quite imaginary—I was prepared to stomach all the vices, the rapes, and the assassinations you might care to mention.[41]

In passages like these, Beauvoir the author built into the volume a continuing, subtle, and unannounced reflection by the narrator, on the character Simone. Thus, the tone substitutes for an introspective discussion on the self, lacking in the volume. Through the repeated use of an ironic tone in the work, the author looks askance at the foolishness of the protagonist. In the other volumes, the direct introspective impulse increases, as we will see.

Memoirs is the story of the production of a liberated life from a constricted, censored, though happily complacent (for the most part) childhood. Beauvoir would later announce that she gave up the project of happiness at the same time she allowed "History" to enter her life. This, it turns out, is a form of "liberation"; liberation is not happiness (as she already noted in Ethics), nor is it complacency and resignation. It is risk—the acknowledgment of one's life as "unfixed," one's self as not an immanence but a transcendence, always skirting immanence, and sometimes nearly being forced into it.

There is also an ironic, sometimes amused and judgmental tone in The Prime of Life, though to a lesser degree than in Memoirs. The reader is prepared by this tone for her claim at the end of Part One that her life was divided again, as it had been in 1929. Since she hadn't discovered her (historical) truth yet, in the years described in the book, 1929–44, she had been living a false life, one from which she distances herself.

Narrating her early years with Sartre, she describes with some ridicule the optimism they shared about their own lives and the progress of the human race, and the sense they had of their own importance: "Man was to be remolded, and the process would be partly our doing. We did not envisage contributing to this change except by way of books: public affairs bored us. We counted on events turning out according to our wishes without any need for us to mix in them personally."[42] At a further point in the volume, as she describes their trip to Spain, she again mocks their youthful pretensions: "Convinced by the books we read that the true quality of a town is to be found only in its poorest quarters, we spent all our evenings down in the Barrio Chino," she says sardonically.[43] Later, relating the time she spent as a young teacher living alone in Marseilles, she emphasizes the seriousness of the young woman intellectual she had been:

That year . . . I gave my life content by a process of self-observation. I was devoted to Katherine Mansfield, the *Journal* and *Letters* no less than the short stories . . . and found her obsessive concept of the "solitary woman" romantically appealing. . . . I told myself that I, too, personified this "solitary woman." . . . I would gaze out at the sky, at the passers-by; then I would lower my eyes to the exercise-books I was correcting or the volume I was reading. I felt wonderful.[44]

Beauvoir's admission of the delight involved in her performance of the "solitary woman" is one more example of the satire she works into her autobiographical narratives. In this case, she exposes to us the romantic fantasies of Simone, the young teacher, even in the face of the mundane "exercise-books" that are the mainstay of a young teacher's life.

This sort of irony crops up through nearly half of *The Prime of Life*.[45] But the work is remarkable for the split within it. Beauvoir structured the book into two parts, to emphasize that her life dramatically changed during these years. As she comes closer and closer to the realization that what she calls "History" is important, the ironic tone lessens. It can only be that Beauvoir begins to recognize herself in the post-1939 woman, and thus the narrator and the protagonist are not as alien to each other. There are two categories by which History makes its mark on her in this volume: the first is the political realm, which she directly claims is the reason for the change in her life; the second is the personal, which she remarks on as important, and also identifies as History.

In regard to the political meaning of the change in her life, it is the rise of fascism in Europe that begins to take its toll on the young romantic, particularly in 1938: "I now passed through one of the most depressing periods of my whole life. I refused to admit that war was even possible, let alone imminent. . . . But the future had begun to open up under my very feet, and produced in me a sick feeling akin to real anguish," she writes.[46] In addition to the growth of fascism, in her own life there were two examples of History: sickness and death. She was seriously ill once, with a painful and dangerous lung infection, and the experience had really shocked her:

as they loaded me into the ambulance I thought, in consternation: "This is really happening, and it's happening to *me*." . . . Now here was a revolution. To be oneself, simply oneself, is so amazing and utterly unique an experience that it's hard to convince oneself so singular a thing happens to everybody in the world, and is amenable to statistics. Sickness, accidents, and misfortunes were things that happened only to other people; but in the eyes of those curious bystanders, I had abruptly become "other people" . . . "This patient they're taking away is *me*," I thought.[47]

Besides being shocked into her mortality and finitude, she had become aware of and depressed by the fact of her aging: "I was getting old. Neither my general health nor my facial appearance bore witness to the fact, but from time to time I felt that everything was going gray and colorless around me, and began to lament the decrepitude of my senses. . . . My curiosity still found matter on which to feed, but there were no more fresh and blinding revelations."[48] Here, Beauvoir makes clear that her sense of growing old is both physical and intellectual. It is because she has "no more fresh and blinding revelations" as well as because she noticed "the decrepitude" of her senses, that she is depressed by her aging.

But it was the understanding of History in the political rather than personal sense which she remarks most on in *Prime of Life*, and which takes her further and further from the playfulness of irony into the dead seriousness that marks *Force of Circumstance* and then, much more so, *All Said and Done*. So important is this change—indeed, it was a "fresh and blinding revelation," those moments that she thought were lost forever to her experience—that she questions narrating the earlier part of her life: "it might be asked, what value is there in the experiences I have now related? Sometimes they seem wrapped in such layers of ignorance and dishonesty that I can feel nothing but contempt for this part of my past life," she wonders.[49] She overcomes the temptation to simply reject it, forming a conclusion about it that is more logical than existential or autobiographical: "Not everything was false."[50] When she began Part Two of *The Prime of Life*, as if to emphasize this change in her life from ignorance to revelation (about History), she begins by including nearly fifty pages of a diary that she began to keep in these years, thus presenting the raw stuff of History as she lived it. The diary form intensifies the force of History, providing the greatest sense of immediacy of any of the forms in which one's memoirs might be written.

In her next autobiographical work, *Force of Circumstance*, which covers the years 1944 to 1962, the reader finds a more serious tone and a more businesslike approach to the material in general. There are thousands of items, personal and political, and thousands of travel facts that need to be related, many of them relevant to Sartre's political career. But there are also many stories of her career as a writer: the genesis of her books, the experience of writing them, and their reception. For example, chapter two begins with one such report, told with economy of detail and precision: "*Blood of Others* was published in September [1945]; its main theme, as I have said, was the paradox of this existence experienced by me as my freedom and by those who came in contact with me as an object. This intention was not apparent to the public; the book was labeled a 'Resistance novel.'"[51] If *Memoirs* was a work about Simone's childhood and *Prime* about her relationship with Sartre and her growing intellectual prowess, *Force of Circumstance* is primarily about her and his writing: philosophical, literary, and political. It relates the breakup of two old friendships over politics, the friendships with Camus and with Merleau-Ponty. It is about other serious matters: sickness and death, but in a much more immediate and somber way than when those subjects came up in *Prime of Life*. It is also the story of an important love affair Sartre had with an American woman, called "M" in the autobiographies, and about Beauvoir's important affairs with Nelson Algren and Claude Lanzmann. One has the impression that, by this time, her relationship with Sartre was close to being a "business and professional partnership" rather than a romantic attachment. She sometimes speaks directly about this:

As always, Sartre was a great help to me. Yet he seemed further away from me than ever before. His successes had not changed him, but he had created a situation which in cutting him off from the world also broke some of our ties; he no longer even set foot in the cafés we had so loved before; he had not followed me down the ski trails at Auron; the unknown partner of our life together had become, by the pressure of circumstances, a public figure. I had the feeling that he had been stolen from me.[52]

This passage might be used as a summary of the volume; the original French includes the volume's title: "*le partenaire inconnu de notre vie à deux était devenu, par la force des choses, un personnage public: j'avais l'impression qu'on me l'avait volé.*"[53] [emphasis added] As she continues this paragraph, however, it becomes clear that the business of life and the seriousness that it brought with it was as much due to *her* choices as to his. She tells us: "he invited me to follow him along his path. 'You should read this!' he would tell me . . . I couldn't; I had to finish my novel."[54]

Of growing concern were health matters; she underwent a breast biopsy for possible cancer, and Sartre's numerous illnesses began in earnest.[55]

About the several serious heath problems that she encountered during this period, beginning in 1957, Beauvoir provides pages from her diary:

Monday, October 6th: Sartre saw the doctor. Tuesday, October 14th: These really are days of horror. . . . Tuesday October 21st: Days of horror. Especially Saturday, when I went to the doctor's. Sunday, yesterday, one long suffocating nightmare! Tuesday, October 28th: Coming out of the nightmare, the illness. I must be already benumbed by old age to be able to bear it. I think I'm going to stop keeping this diary.

And, in fact, I did stop keeping it. I put the pages in a folder, and wrote on it, impulsively: *Diary of a defeat*. And I never touched it again.[56]

The "defeat" was not only sickness and old age; it was also political defeat. A major organizational initiative for the left, embodied in a referendum, that Sartre and Beauvoir had worked a great deal for, was defeated. Beauvoir called it a "sinister defeat because it's not merely the defeat of a party or of an idea, but a repudiation by 80 percent of the French people of all that we had believed in and wanted for France. A repudiation of themselves, an enormous collective suicide."[57] These remarks are a far cry from those playful statements in the very early pages of *The Prime of Life*, with their teasing and self-mocking attitude toward the idealism of Beauvoir and Sartre: "Man was to be remolded, and the process would be partly our doing. We did not envisage contributing to this change except by way of books: public affairs bored us. We counted on events turning out according to our wishes without any need for us to mix in them personally."[58] When explaining how they did contribute by way of "public affairs," in order to "remold" the human race, but particularly the French, the middle-aged Simone de Beauvoir no longer had her sense of irony; she could only state, direly and with more than a hint of sour grapes, that the French had engaged in "an enormous collective suicide."

Introspection is provided but controlled in *Force of Circumstance*; it is excluded from the text for the most part in a formal way by the use of decisive structural elements: an introduction, an interlude, and an epilogue. As a consequence of the organizational decisions Beauvoir made, the text itself is less interesting and challenging to read; it has a journalistic quality in many places, though its introspective statements mentioned above are remarkably sensitive and astute.

The tone of the last volume, *All Said and Done*, is even more serious and lacking in ironic playfulness; it is written as a summary of a life, rather than a story of one, and often is too earnest to be literarily interesting. In this last volume of autobiography, Beauvoir no longer plays the sorts of games with her readers that make any text more challenging. Instead, she thematizes, categorizes, summarizes, and in a way, concludes her life, drawing up her accounts as well as she can (as the title *Tout Compte Fait* indicates, for it also means "all accounts settled"). For example, in the passage in which she discusses her friendship with Violette Leduc, she began by noting the recent death of Leduc, about whom she will speak "under the heading of my living friendships."[59] The reader is a bit startled to learn that one whose "life was closely mingled" with hers will be treated "under the heading" of friendship, or under any heading. This kind of categorization interrupts the narrative; yet in this work, it really *is* the narrative. It does interrupt the ability of the reader to become absorbed in the story of the life of an individual person, however. For example, when she starts relating her trip to Japan with Sartre, she notes it had no "political significance," hence "I am putting it immediately after those trips that I took just for my own pleasure," intentionally excluding her "personal" self from the story of her life; we conclude from this that she is narrating the life of the public figure, "Simone de Beauvoir."[60] With this sort of self-conscious attention to the organization of her life into categories, and to the process of inclusion and exclusion of detail based on the principle of public or political importance, Beauvoir constructs her life story in this volume at a startling distance from her personal self. In fact, the work has the tone of an academic study, with its stress on organization and its reiteration of certain points.

This last volume is largely introspection, since her choice of a structure according to themes and not chronological order forces the reader to confront Beauvoir's self at every turn. In this sense, the volume does have a certain charm that the others do not have; the continual introspective tone of the work leaves the impression of an older but humbler Beauvoir, one who has many more questions than before, in these "concluding pages" of her life. For example, she begins chapter one with a series of questions: "Every morning, even before I open my eyes, I know I am in my bedroom and my bed. But . . . sometimes I wake up with a feeling of childish amazement—why am I myself? What astonishes me, just as it astonishes a child . . . is the fact of finding myself here, and at this moment, deep in this life and not in any other. What stroke of chance has brought this about?"[61] Loaded with questions, this passage is full of curiosity about the self; she asks, "why am I myself?"—the question of an "astonished child"—even as she sums up her accounts. In this passage, she investigates the self directly with as much specificity as anywhere in her autobiographies. Similarly, chapter two opens with questions, as she announces the subject of the chapter, her career of writing: "Writing has remained the great concern of my life. What have my relations with literature been during these last years?"[62]   Chapter three, on her reading, opens with questions also:

When I was a child and an adolescent, reading was not only my favourite pastime, but also the key that opened the world to me. . . . Today both my life and . . . my work are . . . complete . . . no book can possibly bring me any shattering revelation . . . I do ask myself this question: if books can no longer bring me anything decisive, then why am I still so very fond of reading?[63]

Later, when she talks about her travels, another question presents itself: "What have these explorations brought me?"[64] As Beauvoir writes the concluding pages of this work, she continues to ask questions until finally, even though she has said that her life and her work are already accomplished (though the volume was published fourteen years before she died), she announces that she will conclude the book without a conclusion, but rather will leave that to the reader.[65] The final act of this work, to turn the conclusion over to the reader, is in keeping with the nature of the work as a kind of academic exercise. Beauvoir has presented a set of themes, categorized her relationship and activities under these themes, and assumes that, upon presenting this evidence, the serious reader will be able to draw their own conclusions, if they have been good scholars of the evidence.

Beauvoir's choice to leave philosophical writing about the self for autobiographical writing about the self was not a return to philosophical naivete.   The notion of the for-itself, taken from the existential-phenomenological tradition, as well as the notion she developed in *The Second Sex*, which I call "the gendered self," were both used in her autobiographical writings. So, although the self-writing that Beauvoir began with *Memoirs* represented a transfer of field from "philosophy" to "autobiography," it did not represent a renouncing of interest in the development of an understanding of the self.[66]

In "The Book of Margery Kempe," an article about the very first autobiography written in English, Janel Mueller states that the "unique autobiographical design" of Margery Kempe's autobiography is the combination of female spirituality, selfhood, and authorship.[67] By comparison, the unique autobiographical design of Beauvoir's autobiography is the notion of selfhood she presents through the combination of the existential self and the gendered self. Beauvoir problematizes the self into two roles: that which is constrained by genderization, on the one hand, and that which is freed by existentialism. In my chapters on the child, the woman in love, and the writer, I will show how she used both notions of the self, separately and in combination. They remained the ground out of which the discourse on her own self grew. In addition, in the first part of her first volume of autobiography, she provides a *philosophical* foundation for her life story. This means that her autobiographical practice avoids the criticism she makes in *The Second Sex* on the limits of female autobiographers (and most women writers):

When they have removed the veils of illusion and deception, [women writers] think they have done enough; but this negative audacity leaves us still faced by an enigma, for the truth itself is ambiguity, abyss, mystery . . . still too preoccupied with clearly seeing the facts to try to penetrate the shadows. . . . Still amazed at being allowed to explore the phenomena of this world, [women] take inventory without trying to discover meanings. . . . They are interested in things rather than in the relations of things.[68]

In her introductory essay in *The Female Autograph*, Domna Stanton quotes Beauvoir's remarks in *The Second Sex* which are critical of women autobiographers:

Beauvoir chastized the autobiographical narrowness and narcissism of female writing in *The Second Sex*: "it is her own self that is the principal—sometimes the unique subject of interest to [the female autobiographer]." This view had led the future author of five remarkable volumes of memoirs to declare: "there are . . . sincere and engaging feminine autobiographies, but none can compare with Rousseau's *Confessions*" . . . Was this a provocation for women to engage in self-transcending political and philosophical questions or a reflection of the androcentrism of *The Second Sex*?[69]

Though Stanton does not go on to answer this question, it is a good interrogative standpoint from which to begin an in-depth discussion of Beauvoir, writer of autobiography. Without accepting Beauvoir's judgment about women writers, one can say that she took her own advice and set out to produce autobiographical writings that attempted to discover meanings and ask philosophical questions.

Since the philosophical standpoint from which Beauvoir viewed literature, and thus autobiography, was existentialism, her remarks in *The Second Sex* on female autobiographers are followed by what amounts to an existentialist manifesto on creativity (including most importantly, writing); that "Art, literature, philosophy, are attempts to found the world anew on a human liberty: that of the individual creator," but "to entertain such a pretension, one must first unequivocally assume the status of a being who has liberty."[70] But she immediately qualified this existentialist "truth," as required by the comprehensive view she was now taking: "when the struggle to find one's place in this world is too arduous, there can be no question of getting away from it . . . one must first emerge into a sovereign solitude if one wants to try to regain a grasp upon it: what woman needs first of all is to undertake . . . her apprenticeship in abandonment and transcendence: that is, in liberty."[71] By calling for "an apprenticeship in abandonment and transcendence," to be accomplished through "a sovereign solitude," Beauvoir is acknowledging the need for women to be as mobile as men, to be able to move about at will, as well as to have "a room of one's own." The work of the creative artist and thinker requires as much: "Culture must be apprehended through the free action of a transcendence . . . but if a thousand persistent bonds hold it to earth, its surge is broken. To be sure, the young girl can today go out alone and idle in the Tuileries; but I have already noted how hostile the street is to her, with eyes and hands lying in wait everywhere . . . this preoccupation rivets her to the ground and to herself."[72] An *enlightened* existentialism, in this case the Beauvoirian theory that combines it with feminism, will have to take account of both the constraints (including potential violence) placed on the individual due to her gender, and the "innate" liberty of the human being; it will be a comprehensive account which acknowledges limits as much as it praises freedom.

As *The Second Sex* was a study necessary as a preface to her own autobiography, her call for a different kind of female autobiography at the end of *The Second Sex* can be seen as a preface to her own autobiography, one of a specific kind; in which truth, in all of its mystery, will be "unveiled," and meaning will be discovered.

NOTES

1. The terms *introspective* and *retrospective* are used by Paul Jay in *Being in the Text* (Ithaca, NY: Cornell University Press, 1984), p. 24.

2. Hugh J. Silverman, "Sartre's Words on the Self," in *Jean-Paul Sartre: Contemporary Approaches to His Philosophy*, eds. Hugh J. Silverman and Frederick Elliston (Pittsburgh: Duquesne University Press, 1980), p. 87.

3. Terry Keefe, *Simone de Beauvoir: A Study of Her Writings* (Totowa, NJ: Barnes and Noble Books, 1983), p. 44.

4. Simone de Beauvoir, *Adieux: A Farewell to Sartre*, trans. Patrick O'Brian (New York: Pantheon Books, 1984). The French edition was published in 1981.

5. For this general point, see William C. Spengemann, *The Forms of Autobiography* (New Haven: Yale University Press, 1980), pp. 185–6 and 209. Beauvoir repeatedly tells her readers that she has used events from her life in her novels. See, for example, the passages in *The Prime of Life*, pp. 251 and 352.

6. Precisely what is meant by the French term *"littérature"* is also of interest here. I am only noting this system of classification, one which puts *The Ethics of Ambiguity* in the same category as *Memoirs of a Dutiful Daughter.* The meaning of the term *"essai"* is also important. That genre covers a very wide spectrum of works in French literature, so wide a classification as to come close to being a nonclassification. In Sidney D. Braun's *Dictionary of French Literature* (Greenwich, CT: Fawcett Premier Books, 1958), pp. 162–5, he notes that there are many definitions of the essay; "most agree that it ought to be short rather than long, in prose rather than in poetry, and personal or reflective rather than scientific in approach." Braun continues, "Some critics define the essay as a literary work that defies classification and that cannot be called anything else."

7. *Adieux: A Farewell to Sartre* has a remarkable preface, written in the form of direct address to the dead Sartre, stating that this is the only book she would ever write that he hadn't also read. The reader concludes that this book, relating Sartre's last years, would be Beauvoir's last. And it was.

8. Simone de Beauvoir, *Force of Cicumstance*, trans. Richard Howard (New York: Harper Colophon Books, 1977), p. 94. (Hereafter, *Force.*)

9. *Force*, p. 185. Richard Howard's translation is faithful to the original in both places. This quote comes from p. 109 in the French, and the quote in note 7 comes from p. 203 in the French.

10. This work was begun in 1956 and published in 1958. See Keefe, p. 25.

11. Spengemann, p. 62.

12. Philippe Lejeune, *Le Pacte autobiographique* (Paris: Editions du Seuil, 1975), p. 235.

13. Lejeune, pp. 234–5.

14. Lejeune, p. 234.

15. Lejeune, p. 237.

16. Lejeune, p. 200.

17. Simone de Beauvoir, *All Said and Done*, trans. Patrick O'Brian (New York: G. P. Putnam's, 1974), Prologue (pages not numbered).

18. *All Said and Done*, Prologue.

19. Simone de Beauvoir, *The Prime of Life*, trans. Peter Green (Cleveland: World Publishing Company/Meridian Books, 1966), p. 178. (Hereafter, *Prime.*)

20. *Prime*, p. 9.

21. Simone de Beauvoir, *Memoirs of a Dutiful Daughter*, trans. James Kirkup (New York: Harper Colophon Books, 1974), p. 360. (Hereafter, *Memoirs.*)

22. *Prime*, p. 10.

23. *Force*, p. 463.

24. *Force*, pp. 390 and 413.

25. *Prime*, p. 9.

26. *Force*, p. v.

27. *Force*, p. v.

28. *Force*, p. 273.

29. *Force*, p. 274.

30. This is a curious notion. Philippe Lejeune's criticism of her autobiography, discussed earlier, calls attention to this attitude. See Lejeune, pp. 199–200, 234–7.

31. *All Said and Done*, Prologue.

32. Simone de Beauvoir, *Tout compte fait* (Paris: Gallimard, 1972), p. 10.

33. Lejeune also has remarked on this point in his work, cited above. I discuss this later.

34. Others have remarked on this also. See Keefe, pp. 32–3.

35. *Memoirs*, p. 27.

36. *Memoirs*, p. 27.

37. *Memoirs*, p. 27.

38. *Memoirs*, pp. 172–3.

39. *Memoirs*, p. 182.

40. *Memoirs*, p. 182.

41. *Memoirs*, p. 195.

42. *Prime*, p. 18.

43. *Prime*, p. 71.

44. *Prime*, p. 85.

45. Referring to her strange intimidation by Simone Weil, Beauvoir remarks that she often used irony to cope with the intimidation, explaining, "I could not absorb her into my universe, and this seemed to constitute a vague threat to me. . . . I refused to envisage other people as potential individuals, with consciences, like myself. I would not put myself in their shoes; and that was one reason for my addiction to irony." *Prime*, p. 105–6.

46. *Prime*, pp. 254–6.

47. *Prime*, p. 233.

48. *Prime*, p. 168.

49. *Prime*, p. 289.

50. *Prime*, p. 289.

51. *Force*, p. 37.

52. *Force*, p. 255.

53. Simone de Beauvoir, *La Force des choses* (Paris: Gallimard, 1963), p. 275. It is curious that the translator doesn't use the title of the volume when he translates this; it would make the strong connection that Beauvoir undoubtedly wanted to make at this point in the narrative with this stage of her life.

54. *Force*, p. 255.

55. *Force*, p. 258.

56. *Force*, pp. 450–1.

57. *Force*, p. 449.

58. *Prime*, p.18.

59. *All Said and Done*, p. 47.

60. *All Said and Done*, p. 251.

61. *All Said and Done*, p. 1.

62. *All Said and Done*, p. 114.

63. *All Said and Done*, p. 138.

64. *All Said and Done*, p. 212.

65. *All Said and Done*, p. 463.

66. Postmodernist and deconstructionist thinking (e.g., the writings of Michel Foucault and Jacques Derrida) problematizes such boundaries between the genres or the disciplines. These discussions are relevant here, though I don't take them up in this work.

67. Janel Mueller, "Autobiography of a 'New Creatur': Female Spirituality, Selfhood, and Authorship in 'The Book of Margery Kempe,'" in *The Female Autograph*, ed. Domna C. Stanton (Chicago: University of Chicago Press, 1987), p. 59.

68. Simone de Beauvoir, *The Second Sex*, trans. H. M. Parshley (New York: Vintage, 1989), p. 710.

69. Domna C. Stanton, "Autogynography: Is the Subject Different?" in *The Female Autograph: Theory and Practice of Autobiography from the Tenth to the Twentieth Century* (Chicago: University of Chicago Press, 1987), p. 5.

70. *The Second Sex*, p. 711.

71. *The Second Sex*, p. 711.

72. *The Second Sex*, p. 712.

4

Writing the Self: The Child

Some claim that childhood autobiography is a separate genre. Richard Coe, in *When the Grass Was Taller*, laments the fact that it has remained at least unlabeled, if not completely unacknowledged by English language critics. He notes that German scholars had coined a single word for it—*Jugenderinnerungen*—as early as the eighteenth century. A little later, French critics began referring to it as *souvenirs d'enfance*.[1]

Using this principle of classification, Beauvoir's *Memoirs* should be read separately from her other autobiographical works (Coe discusses *Memoirs* in his book). Though it has a stronger narrative line than the others, with a more self-conscious beginning and ending, Beauvoir's *Memoirs* (unlike most of the autobiographies Coe discusses), was followed by several other autobiographical works. In that regard, Beauvoir's autobiography belongs to a category that Coe defines as an "exasperating hybrid" (a category that includes George Sand's *Histoire de ma vie*):

> If there is an awkward category which seems to defy the "rules," it is perhaps that which we might call the "multi-storeyed Childhood"—that is, autobiographies of enormous length and . . . in several volumes each published separately, of which the first one, two, or more volumes, each complete in itself, deal specifically with childhood and adolescence, but are followed by later volumes concerning themselves with adult life.[2]

According to Coe, virtually all such "multi-storeyed" autobiographies are not truly autobiographies; they are "memoirs," meaning "recollections of others rather than of the self." In his opinion, however, *Memoirs* is a true autobiography, though Beauvoir's only one.[3] A system of genre classification (either pure or hybrid) such as Coe uses, is not particularly helpful here, nor can it be defended easily. I prefer to connect the philosophical issues that interested the thinker and writer, Simone de Beauvoir, throughout her writings, rather than segregate isolated parts of her autobiographical work from other parts of it. The problems such an approach as Coe's creates are immediately obvious. When he discusses the young Simone's original understanding of the inevitability and universality of death, he finds he must also take account of the existentialist writer, Beauvoir:

The problem here, of course, is to distinguish between *the original experience and that experience refashioned in the telling by the adult already trained in a specific form of philosophical expression.* The impression that there is at least a firm foundation of *authentic experience* is strengthened by the manner in which identical reactions are expressed by [those] who are anything but existentialist in outlook or in vocabulary.[4][italics added]

The autobiographies of both Sartre and Beauvoir have authenticity, in Coe's judgment, because they present evidence of archetypal experiences of childhood which many other writers of childhood autobiographies share. But Coe's dichotomy between the authentic and the philosophical can hardly be helpful in understanding Beauvoir's or Sartre's autobiographies, where one continually confronts existentialism. Coe defends his position by claiming that the *authentic* archetypal experiences of childhood are *existential*, rather than merely social.[5] Without any specific definition of terms, Coe claims that Beauvoir's and Sartre's autobiographies are authentic because they are experientially "existential," but not very philosophically existentialist; any philosophical existentialism they exhibit is founded on a deeper, experiential existentialism. How can a reader ever conclude this, I wonder?

ESSENTIAL AND EXISTENTIAL MOMENTS

In the opening pages of *The Second Sex*, published before *Memoirs*, Beauvoir makes the announcement that she will present a rejection of essentialism in favor of an existentialist analysis of woman. Essentialism is the notion that human beings have a fixed and determinate nature, fixed in advance of any choices made by the individual.

But very early in *Memoirs*, Beauvoir claims that in fact essentialism was the primary worldview which she grew up accepting from all of the adults around her: parents, grandparents, and her nurse. Here, she introduces highly charged conceptual terminology, terminology which had already been discredited by existentialism, to explain how she was raised:

The two major *categories* into which my universe was divided were Good and Evil. I inhabited the region of the good, where happiness and virtue reigned in indissoluble unity. . . . A sword of fire separated good from evil. . . . Evil kept a respectful distance. I could imagine its *agents* only as mythical figures like the Devil . . . not having encountered them in the flesh, I reduced them to pure *essences*. . . . All my experience belied this *essentialism*. . . . Whatever I beheld with my own eyes and every real experience had to be fitted somehow or other into a rigid *category*: the *myths* and the *stereotyped ideas* prevailed over the *truth*: unable to pin it down, I allowed truth to dwindle into insignificance.[6] [italics added]

When she distanced herself from essentialism in *The Second Sex* she also, therefore, distanced herself from her childhood. The distancing from her childhood that she achieved philosophically through her part in the development of existentialism, and through her application of existentialism to women in the analysis she made in *The Second Sex*, was further achieved through the writing of her autobiography. It was from her parents, her nursemaid Louise, and other adults around her, that she received a Manichaean view of the world. But in the above summary she made of that period, the philosophical language she uses ("categories," "agents," "essences," "essentialism," "ideas") was more sophisticated than Manichaeism required. In addition, though *Memoirs* was conceived before *The Second Sex* but not written before it, we can trace the influence of the latter in this passage also; her mention of "the myths and the sterotyped ideas" reflects the analysis Beauvoir made in *The Second Sex* in regard to women.

Within this passage, Beauvoir relates two closely connected events that indicate the effect of this essentialism in her life and the break with it that she began to make. The first concerned a scolding her mother gave to Louise. What shocked Simone was not simply the scolding, but the emotional interaction between the two women: "She [Mama] was the oldest, and she was 'Madame,' so she had the right to scold Louise; but I didn't like the look of her mouth or the tone of her voice; I didn't like to see something that wasn't friendliness in Louise's patient eyes."[7] This animosity between two of the "good" was incomprehensible to her. Very soon after, she was with Louise and another adult in the garden when they overheard an argument in the house between Simone's parents: "'There's Monsieur and Madame fighting again,' said Louise. That was when my universe began to totter. It was impossible that papa and mama should be enemies, that Louise should be their enemy; when the impossible happened, heaven was confused with hell, darkness was conjoined with light. I began to drown in the chaos which preceded creation."[8] It is most likely that these were not two isolated incidents, but that Simone had finally allowed herself to begin to "see" ("I didn't like to see something that wasn't friendliness in Louise's patient eyes") and to begin to hear ("There's Monsieur and Madame fighting again") in order to begin to create her self, through "the chaos which preceded creation." The essentialism she learned and then disavowed was often couched heavily in religious notions. Not only did she learn it that way, but as she related it later, the religious notions, or at least the terminology, continued in how she narrated it, as in her remark that she consigned Louise's remarks about her parents to "the limbo of forgetfulness" (where presumably they awaited the Last Judgment Day, the writing of her autobiography).[9]

Another alarming incident involving Louise and her mother followed. Talking to a neighbor's maid, Louise criticized Simone's mother's dress ("eccentric") and her singing voice ("screaming like a macaw").[10] The discord between her mother and Louise indicated by these remarks greatly troubled Simone:

Eccentric. Macaw. These words sounded awful to me: what had they to do with Mama, who was beautiful, elegant, and sang and played so well? And yet it was Louise who had used them: how could I counter their sinister power? I knew how to defend myself against other people: but Louise! She was justice in person; she was truth itself, and my respect for her forbade me to pass judgement on anything she said. . . . I should have had to admit that she did not get on well with Mama; in which case, one of them must be in the wrong about something! No. I wanted to have them both perfect.[11]

There was a twofold process in the way she chose to cope with imperfection in two of the three beings she called "those supreme divinities—Louise and my parents—who alone could be infallible."[12] She cultivated a new awareness of both her mother's taste in clothes and her vocal ability and less deference toward Louise's pronouncements: "From then on, whenever Mama wore a new dress or sang at the top of her voice, I always felt a certain uneasiness. Moreover, knowing now that it wouldn't do to attach too much importance to what Louise had to say, I no longer listened to her with quite the same docility as before."[13] This indicates that early on Beauvoir had begun the rejection of essentialism that was a necessary if not sufficient condition for an existentialist, in spite of her own claims to the contrary, for she says ungenerously of herself at this period: "Whatever I beheld with my own eyes and every real experience had to be fitted somehow or other into a rigid category: the myths and the stereotyped ideas prevailed over the truth."[14] That may have been true of her at three or four years old; by five and a half, it seems, she was giving the truth its due, while also making whatever adjustments were necessary to survive.

As she describes the use of Manichaeism in her own upbringing, she claims that her own perceptions of the world were more subtle than those presented by the adults around her, who insisted on a simplified world. Particularly in relation to words, this became an issue, which she discusses on more than one occasion in *Memoirs:*

All my experience belied this essentialism. White was only rarely totally white, and the blackness of evil was relieved by lighter touches; I saw greys and half-tones everywhere. Only as soon as I tried to define their muted shades, I had to use words, and I found myself in a world of bony-structured concepts. . . . When [the grown-ups] defined a thing, they expressed its substance, in the sense in which one expresses the juice from a fruit. So that I could conceive of no gap into which error might fall between the word and its object; that is why I submitted myself uncritically to the Word, without examining its meaning, even when circumstances inclined me to doubt its truth.[15]

In her experience, reality was complex, but her own perceptions were invalidated by the extreme simplification and rigid categorization imposed by her parents and other adults; consequently, "the myths and the stereotyped ideas prevailed over the truth."[16]

In *The Prime of Life,* describing an intellectual disagreement between herself and Sartre (rare at this point in their relationship), she again assesses the power of words against the richness of reality:

I maintained that reality extends beyond anything that can be said about it; that instead of reducing it to symbols capable of verbal expression, we should face it as it is—full of ambiguities, baffling, and impenetrable. Sartre replied that anyone who wished, as we did, to arrange the world in a personal pattern must do something more than observe and react; he must grasp the meaning of phenomena and pin them down in words. . . . This split between us was to continue for a long time: my own prime allegiance was to life, to the here-and-now reality, while for Sartre literature came first. Still, since I wanted to write and he enjoyed living, we seldom came into open conflict.[17]

The drive to abstract reality into categories in written form, a process that was more comfortable to Sartre, conflicted with Beauvoir's desire at this point in her life to "let being be," to not disturb reality by crafting it into something else, but to immerse oneself in the stream of it. In *The Second Sex,* Beauvoir had criticized women writers for being content to represent reality rather than understand or interpret it anew: "they are still too concerned with [clear-sightedness] . . . to discover meanings . . . they present their experience, still warm . . . they are interested in things rather than in the relations of things," she had said.[18] The self she presents to the reader in the previous passage from *The Prime of Life* resembles this *woman* writer, a gendered self whom she criticizes for fleeing the creation of meaning, content with merely expressing "life." Though she makes no such connection for us in the passage, we may note the connection anyway.

In later attempts to free herself from essentialism, Simone sometimes took absurd stands. In *The Prime of Life*, Beauvoir relates an incident in 1934 in which, in an attempt to deny essentialism, she forced herself to take a naively reductionist position:

One day [Olga] asked what it *really* meant to be a Jew. With absolute certainty I replied: "Nothing at all. There are no such things as 'Jews'; only human beings." . . . in reaction against my father's ideologies, I objected when people talked to me about Frenchmen, Germans, or Jews: for me there were only individuals. I was right to reject essentialism; I knew already what abuses could follow in the train of abstract concepts such as . . . the "Jewish character," . . . But the universalist notions to which I turned bore me equally far from reality.[19]

Her rejection of essentialism was accomplished by the time she wrote *The Second Sex*. In that book's introduction, she rejected "femininity" and "Jewishness," but in a more enlightened way than she did with her student in the scene described; "To decline to accept such notions as the eternal feminine, the black soul, the Jewish character, is not to deny that Jews, Negroes, women exist today—this denial does not represent a liberation for those concerned, but rather a flight from reality," she remarked.[20]

Essentialism had fashioned a view of the whole world, not merely the human being, a world "harmoniously based on fixed coordinates and divided into clear-cut compartments."[21] This is probably what she is referring to later in *La Force de l'âge* (*The Prime of Life*) when she says, "there were occasions when . . . my old nostalgia for the absolute would reappear."[22] (This is my translation. Peter Green translates it as "my old hankering after the Absolute," but this is misleading, as it connotes theism and mysticism. When she says "my old nostalgia for the absolute," I believe she is referring to human attempts to fix and define the "truth," to compartmentalize the world, and to arrest the continual creation of meaning, her *modus operandi* in the essentialist days of her childhood. As a young adult, her "nostalgia for the absolute" would clearly have amounted to an attempt to deny her newfound philosophical and personal understanding of, and appreciation for "existence," for the serenity of "essence.")

As Beauvoir describes it in the passage quoted earlier, this essentialism was allied with a cosmic Manichaeism: "The two major categories into which my universe was divided were Good and Evil. I inhabited the region of the good. . . . A sword of fire separated good from evil."[23] This Manichaean essentialism was also previewed in the description of childhood that she had presented earlier in *The Ethics of Ambiguity*: "Rewards, punishments . . . instill in [the child] the conviction that there exist a good and evil which like a sun and a moon exist as ends in themselves."[24] Another important use of Manichaeism occurs in *The Second Sex*; there Beauvoir was critical of Manichaeism, as well as essentialism. Manichaeism first appears in the epigraph to the first volume, in the form of a quotation attributed to Pythagoras, and at numerous places in the text as an underlying concept for the analysis of woman's role in civilization.[25] The quotation reads: "There is a good principle which created order, light, and man and an evil principle which created chaos, darkness, and woman."[26]

The moral correlate of the division of the world into good and evil was that good was to be sought and evil avoided. One of the forms this took was the censorship of Simone's reading, when she was a child. This censorship was an ongoing activity performed with great care by her parents, especially by her mother, from her very early childhood. The books chosen for her were always representative of the extremely rigid and conventional moral standards held by her parents and teachers, works in which "the good were rewarded, and the wicked punished."[27] Simone accepted her parents' version of the world, though on reflection she was aware of how narrow it was; "it would be impossible to imagine a more sectarian education than the one I received," she says.[28]

Simone found a way out of the Manichaean trap in a moment of personal revelation brought on by her father's calamitous prophecies that evil would be victorious. Because this amounted to prophecies of future worldwide destruction, young Simone felt personally threatened by this doomsaying: "this future that he painted in such lurid colours was *my* future; I loved life: I couldn't accept that tomorrow it would be filled with hopeless lamentation. One day . . . I hit upon an answer: 'Whatever happens,' I said, 'it will be men who win the final victory.' . . . The Other Side . . . suddenly ceased to appear as Evil incarnate (*le Mal absolu*) . . . I breathed again."[29] When she decided that her father's depictions of two sides, good and evil, were reducible to one—humanity—it meant that in the end, regardless of which side won, human beings would win. For the time being, she needn't fight for *her* way of seeing things; she could relax in the knowledge that, regardless of which side was victorious, humans would be victorious and that meant that she had a future and was saved from despair.

LANGUAGE, LITERATURE, AND THE FREE SELF

The books and stories provided by her parents never reflected reality as she knew it. They were carefully selected to reflect the metaphysical and moral view of her parents; their astute daughter knew that the world those books depicted was an unrealistic one. There, goodness was rewarded, evil punished: "I did not try to find any relationship between reality and the fantasies I read in books," Beauvoir wrote.[30] Yet there was a positive result of this censorship, for Simone came to understand in a profound way that a story is a fabrication for the reader's entertainment: "I was aware of the necessity informing these constructions which have a beginning, a development, and an end, and in which words and phrases shine with their own peculiar radiance, like colours in a picture. . . . The thing that amused me was to manipulate an object through the use of words, as I once used to make constructions with building-blocks."[31] In turn, this resulted in a strong dichotomy forming in her mind between literature and life. Consequently, she modeled her own childhood writing on other people's writing, not on life. "I never had the idea that I might write down my own experiences or even my dreams," she says.[32]

It was only much later, when she was seventeen and a young college student, upon discovering contemporary French literature (the works of Claudel, Valéry, Gide) that literature became connected to reality for her:

suddenly, men of flesh and blood were speaking to me with their lips close to my ear; it was something between them and me; they were giving expression to the aspirations and the inner rebellions which I had never been able to put in words, but which I recognized. . . . Literature took the place in my life that had once been occupied by religion; it absorbed me entirely, and transfigured my life.[33]

Since this type of literature was not among the ranks of the works of the literary good, it fell into the category of evil for Simone's parents. Her passion for it became the occasion of additional conflict with them.[34] In *The Ethics of Ambiguity* Beauvoir had noted that certain times in the life of an individual are most conducive to the assumption of freedom. She claimed that adolescence is such a privileged time, that is, when the opportunity for moral choice really appears for the first time, and when freedom first reveals itself.[35] One of the subjects Beauvoir uses in *Memoirs* to show connections between Simone's awareness of limits on her self and the steps she took to correct the situation is the ongoing censorship of her reading by her parents. As she reached the age of puberty, she became aware that more and more of her actions and judgments were out of the bounds set by her parents: "I accepted their verdicts while at the same time I looked upon myself with other eyes than theirs. *My* essential self (*la vérité de mon être*) still belonged to them as much as to me: but paradoxically the self (*ma vérité*) they knew could only be a decoy now; it could be false."[36] She decided to continue to make her own judgments, against her parents', but at the same time realized an ongoing need for secretive behavior. Therefore, she began to clandestinely read the censored books in her parents' library when she could, while continuing to value her own ability to judge right from wrong in such matters: "From my own point of view, there was nothing reprehensible in my conduct . . . my parents were anxious about my well-being: I was not going against their wishes because my reading wasn't doing me any harm," she noted.[37] This change was accompanied by important changes in others also: her father's dislike for her ungainly appearance, a decrease in her sister's worshipful behavior toward her, and her mother's suspicion of the changes she sensed in Simone. Though forming a newer, freer self, Simone was still "between selves" at puberty, with the discomfort that entailed: "I was uncertain of myself (*moi-même*) and vulnerable."[38]

In Book Three of *Memoirs*, when Beauvoir describes her struggle with her parents over the new books and new values she was being introduced to during her college studies at the Institut Sainte-Marie, along with the formation of her new ideas, she once again remarks on the use of language to formulate a world and, thereby, control the flow of ideas. Up to this point, her parents thought themselves correct in designing a version of the world for her and attempting to enforce it, with all its limitations. She says: "It would be impossible to imagine a more sectarian education. . . . School primers, text books, lessons . . . converged upon the same point. I was never allowed to hear, even at a great distance, even very faintly, the other side of the question."[39] Prior to her conscious awareness of this parental manipulation, Simone had lived the life of what Herbert Marcuse called (following Hegel) the "Happy Consciousness": "the belief that the real is rational and that the system delivers the goods."[40] When she began to discover that her own class, and her own parents, who had always encouraged her to develop her intellectual skills, were in fact part of a value system tied to the interests of the bourgeois class, not to the needs of individuals or humanity as a whole, she felt betrayed: "I had fallen into a trap; the bourgeoisie had persuaded me that its interests were closely linked with those of humanity as a whole; I thought that I could enlist the support of my own class in the pursuit of truths that would be valid for everyone . . . gradually my resentment turned to open rebell-ion."[41] From this feeling of betrayal, Simone moved from acceptance to rebellion, and from "Happy Consciousness" to "Unhappy Consciousness." Up to this point she had always found ways to adapt to the censorship of her reading and ideas, but now she was no longer able to adapt. Her understanding at that point in her life of what she calls "*l'oppression du langage*" was an understanding of the function of authority, of which censorship is a subset, and how language serves authority.[42] Her parents thought themselves correct in designing a version of the world for her and attempting to enforce it, with all its limitations, so that she was never exposed to both sides of any question.

As we saw earlier, she had always been particularly sensitive to this "tyranny of language," and at this crisis point with her parents, she claims to have understood its function. Her description of the parent-child language dynamic is as harsh as it is metaphysical:

As soon as I opened my mouth I provided them with a stick to beat me with, and once more I would be shut up in that world which I had spent years trying to get away from, in which everything, without any possibility of mistake, has its own name, its set place and its agreed function, in which hate and love, good and evil are as crudely differentiated as black and white, in which from the start everything is classified, catalogued, fixed and formulated, and irrevocably judged.[43]

Even earlier in *Memoirs* she had connected the force of "words," "the tyranny of language," with adult commands and the presence of authority in her life. There she relates her tendency toward tantrums as a child. In a particularly insightful and compelling passage, she describes how a perfectly bright and well-liked little girl rebels to the point of hysteria:

I had fits of rage during which my face turned purple and I would fall to the ground in convulsions. I am three and a half years old . . . I am given a red plum and I begin to peel it. "No," says Mama; and I throw myself howling on the ground . . . I have often wondered what were the causes of these outbursts, and what significance they had. . . . I refused to submit to *that intangible force: words*. The arbitrary nature of the *orders and prohibitions* against which I beat unavailing fists was to my mind proof of their inconsistency; yesterday I peeled a peach; then why couldn't I peel a plum? I knew myself beaten; but I wouldn't give in. I fought my losing battle to the bitter end . . . engulfed in the rising dark of my own helplessness; nothing was left but my naked *self* that exploded in prolonged howls and screams .[44] [italics added]

In passages like this, Beauvoir is intent to tell the reader that her open rebellion with her parents often took the form of a rebellion about words, language, and/or books. One can infer the presence of the serious world described in *The Ethics of Ambiguity* also. One of the ways the serious appears in the child's world (where the adults are divinities) is as force, because with the beginning of the development of the child's subjectivity, in the desire to choose for one's self (to peel a plum), what seemed like givens are exposed as actions of force, as wills of other individuals subjecting the child (Simone) to their own will. With the realization that her own will is in contest with another's, her "naked self" emerges. The intentional for-itself becomes real, making its own choices, yet still lacking the power to carry them through; in these tantrums, these little battles, the child Simone was battling for her self. But these excursions into selfhood were terminated—or sublimated—about the age of six, when finally Simone surrendered her early fight for independence and metamorphosized into a good little girl for many years: "I had composed the personality I wished to present to the world; it had brought me so much praise and so many great satisfactions that I had finished by identifying myself with the character I had built up: it was my one reality. . . . For some time, I was to be the docile reflection of my parents' will."[45] Readers of *Memoirs* might want to dispute her claim of docility, but in any case the bulk of the book is meant to be both a narration of that self which is a "docile reflection" of the will of others, a self not yet able to assume its freedom, and the story of the genesis of a self who would become liberated from that.

Beauvoir acknowledges her own sensitivity to the "tyranny of language," connecting it with force, since through language her parents or their representatives had issued commands. The use of tangible power, which could and sometimes did result in physical control and punishment, began with language; "I refused to submit to that intangible force: words. . . . Why must I stop playing just at that particular moment? I seemed to be confronted everywhere by force, never by necessity," she stated.[46] In early childhood parental control of language had defined her world, as well as merely censoring and controlling it:

I assumed that [language] was an exact equivalent of reality; I was encouraged in this misconception by the grown-ups . . . the sole depositaries of absolute truth: when they defined a thing, they expressed its substance, in the sense in which one expresses the juice from a fruit . . . I submitted myself uncritically to the Word, without examining its meaning, even when circumstances inclined me to doubt its truth.[47]

This is in strong contrast to how she credits her parents' moralistic controls with her literary ability to understand the difference between fiction and reality. Guarded by divine parental beings, Simone's earliest world was a Garden of Eden before the fall. Beginning in childish rages against parental proscriptions, her fall continued erratically until it developed seriously with her enrollment in the Institut Sainte-Marie, and it was completed with the death of her good friend Zaza, an event which also marks the end of *Memoirs*.

ETHICAL ESCAPES

Memoirs ends in 1929 when Beauvoir is twenty-one, a year that marks her escape from the fate laid out for her.[48] It also was the year of the death of Zaza, Elisabeth Le Coin, for not all of those who fight against their fate will gain the "victorious release."[49] One's comrades may fall in battle, thereby underscoring the life/death struggle that freedom entails and its precious and costly nature. *Memoirs* ends with her assertion that she fought—along with Zaza—against their "revolting fate."[50] In the preface of the next volume, *The Prime of Life*, Beauvoir fastens on the centrality of freedom to her; "Freedom I had—but freedom to do what? What new direction would the course of my life take as a result of this . . . pitched battle that had culminated in victorious release?" she says.[51]

Beauvoir chose to end these first memoirs with the claims of a battle being fought and won. As author, she chose to use in the book's title the word "*rangée*," a word that carries both "embattled" and "well brought up," and she begins her second volume with the reminder that indeed it was a battle—for life, in her case, and to the death, in the case of Zaza. Having achieved her freedom from the "revolting fate" designed for her by her family and her class, in *The Prime of Life*, Beauvoir tells us she turned toward the future in the realization of freedom, the freedom of the for-itself. "Freedom . . . What new direction would the course of my life take?" she asked, as she approached the task of explaining how this existentialist writer had earlier chosen to live her life.[52]   She takes seriously her claim in *The Ethics of Ambiguity* that freedom is not a state inherited or given, but rather earned.[53] It is what a self may achieve, if that self fights against thinghood by asserting that it *is* freedom, with a future of its own choosing, not a thing with a fate created by others nor by conditions.

In *Ethics*, Beauvoir's formulations of the self move between an "is" and an "ought." In *Force of Circumstance*, she relates that she wrote *Ethics* because she believed one could base a morality on *Being and Nothingness* if one converted the simple desire to *be* into an assumption of existence.[54] The "ought" begins with the claim that one must will freedom by positively assuming the freedom that the for-itself is and has.[55]   By the book's middle, however, and to the end, an important addition takes place; the willing of one's own freedom is intricately bound up with that of others, because one is defined only through her "relationship to the world and to other individuals."[56] This move, from the freedom of the for-itself to the insistence on the relation of it to the freedom of others, is a strong departure from Sartre's *Being and Nothingness*. (It is important to note here that he called his work an ontology and not an ethics.[57])

The philosophical proposition that individuals achieve their freedom only through the freedom of others (that is, the assertion of the interconnectedness of human freedom) may be what led Beauvoir to make the last, haunting remark in *Memoirs*—about Zaza: "She has often appeared to me at night . . . seeming to gaze reproachfully at me. . . . for a long time I believed that I had paid for my own freedom with her death," she says.[58] Beauvoir wrote this about an event that took place in 1929, before she published *Ethics*. However, we have no way of knowing when she began believing this, nor do we know when she came to the opinion of the interconnectedness of human freedom, nor indeed, which caused which. The death of Zaza and her own seemingly misplaced, illogical sense of guilt at being both alive and free may have been significant in leading her to her claim of the interconnectedness of human freedom in *Ethics*. When reading certain passages in *Ethics*, one tends to think of struggles of masses on the national and international front against oppressors, not of a struggle on the individual level; nor does one tend to interpret such a remark by thinking that one friend who achieved freedom (if another failed to) may have felt some guilt. But Beauvoir's guilt is particularly strange, since she had made a clear decision, in advance of Zaza's death, that she would do all she could to support her attempt to escape; "I had decided to fight with all my strength to prevent her life becoming a living death," she said.[59] Instead it became an actual death.

Zaza died in the midst of a romantic agony created by her family's refusal to let her marry Maurice Merleau-Ponty ("Pradelle" in *Memoirs*).[60] Though there were physical diagnoses of the cause of her death (meningitis or encephalitis), Beauvoir was unconvinced. She wondered: "Had it been a contagious disease, or an accident? Or had Zaza succumbed to exhaustion and anxiety?"[61] Regardless of what the real cause of Zaza's death was, in this story Beauvoir recognized that, years prior to her own extension of the Sartrean notion of the self into an ethics, she held a notion of the interconnectedness of human freedom, of the claim she would make that "to will oneself free is also to will others free."[62] Zaza's death, or to be more explicit, Zaza's corpse, is the foundation on which *Memoirs* was written; the corpse underwrites the autobiography, as Beauvoir's self-life-writing becomes connected to the death of the other, as all selves are radically connected to others in life, according to Beauvoirian existentialism.[63]

In *Memoirs* Beauvoir often presents the protagonist Simone as the One and Only, a sovereign individual, recognizable in existentialist theory and created by definition against another individual, her sister. It was in relation to her sister that she defined herself, since her sister was her equal, but one to whom, paradoxically, Simone was superior.

Simone's early years were marked by a relationship with her sister Hélène, nicknamed Poupette (Little Doll), two and a half years younger and her only sibling, in which the elder's importance was continuously underlined; she states, "I was, it appears, very jealous, but not for long. As far back as I can remember, I was always proud of being first. . . . I had a little sister: that doll-like creature (*poupon*) didn't have me."[64]

The two sisters were treated with exaggerated fairness and many external signs of equality, though the family was disappointed that the second child was not a boy. Simone was confident of her own greater importance in numerous ways: "I had never been compared with anyone: she was always being compared with me," she says, and further, "It is plain that I only thought of her as being 'the same, but different,' which is one way of claiming one's preeminence."[65] Beauvoir claims that the sisters got along well, though the reader can easily wonder whether the younger sister was served as well by the arrangement: "she was my liegeman, my *alter ego*, my double; we could not do without one another."[66] The games they played were the products of Simone's imagination; "I was always the one who expressed myself through them; I imposed them upon my sister, assigning her the minor roles which she accepted with complete docility," she says.[67] Not only because of the games and fantasies that they shared, but because of the master/pupil relationship they established (Poupette the willing pupil, Simone the teacher), Simone found herself empowered in a way that adults could not—or would not—empower her; they would only humor her.

Simone's sense of empowerment was accompanied by a sense of freedom, though it was a freedom accomplished to some extent at her sister's expense. "Thanks to my sister I was asserting my right to personal freedom; she was my accomplice, my subject, my creature," she wrote.[68] Fostered by her sister's studious attention, Simone's emerging self gained importance; "When I started to change ignorance into knowledge . . . I felt I was . . . breaking away from the passivity of childhood and entering the great human circle in which everyone is useful to everyone else,"[69] she notes. Becoming real by making its mark on the world, "breaking away from the passivity of childhood," the for-itself takes its place in "the great human circle in which everyone is useful to everyone else." The sovereign self marks itself not in a territorial way, but because it is useful. It exists insofar as it becomes active in the world, but active in work that connects each of us to others by our needs and our skills.

BEING-TOWARDS-DEATH

There are two significant passages in *Memoirs* on the child Simone's awareness of death. They are of interest to the discussion of the existential self since the topic of death, the awareness of death, and the anxiety over it hold an important place in existential philosophy. They differ markedly because in the first, Simone is aware of the effect of death on those close to the dead. In the second, Simone becomes thoroughly aware of the inevitability of her own death. Both passages illustrate the notion of the existentialist self.

In the first passage, Beauvoir relates the death of the infant child of her former nursemaid, Louise, beginning with a visit she made to Louise's home—in a garret—when the baby was born. She was shocked at the conditions in which they lived, "a universe in which the air you breathed smelt of soot, in which no ray of light ever penetrated the filth and squalor: existence here was a slow *death*" [italics added].[70] Shortly after, Louise's baby died; Simone was further distraught, as one form of death was followed by another: "I cried for hours: it was the first time I had known misfortune at first hand. I thought of Louise in her comfortless garret without her baby, without anything . . . 'It's not right!' I told myself. I wasn't only thinking of the dead child but also of that sixth-floor landing. But in the end I dried my tears without having called society in question."[71] Yet it is apparent that she did call society into question at this point, since an awareness of economic injustice was part of her memory of the event. This same event, the death of Louise's baby, was used in two other writings by Beauvoir: in the novel, *The Blood of Others*, and in the essay, *Pyrrhus et Cinéas*. In *The Blood of Others* (originally published in 1945), Jean, the male protagonist, born into a bourgeois family and nearly overcome with bourgeois guilt throughout the novel (to the point of being tiresome to the other characters, as well as to the reader), is distraught at the death of the child of "Louise," a character not mentioned before this passage. Writing the fictional version of the story more than ten years before the autobiographical version, Beauvoir presents a similar but more dramatic version of the incident than she did in *Memoirs*, as Jean recollects his childhood:

> I was eight years old when for the first time I came face to face with the original evil. . . . [when] my mother . . . said: "Louise's baby is dead." Once again I see the twisted staircase . . . Mother told me that behind every door there was a room in which a whole family lived. We went in. Louise took me in her arms . . . In the cradle was a white-faced baby with closed eyes . . . I began to cry. I was crying, Mother was talking, and the baby remained dead. In vain could I empty my money-box . . . it would always be just as dead.[72]

The child Jean is temporarily forced from his sadness by his father's command to stop his mourning. Yet soon he is overtaken again by it, and by the guilt that accompanied it: "Louise's baby is dead. . . . I cried myself to sleep because of that thing . . . more bitter than the sense of guilt—my sin. The sin of smiling while Louise was weeping, the sin of shedding my own tears and not hers. The sin of being another being."[73]

In *Pyrrhus et Cinéas* (written in 1944), Beauvoir makes her first use of this experience: "I knew a child who cried because the son of her concierge died; her parents let her cry and then they became irritated. 'After all, this little boy wasn't your brother.' . . . But in that was a dangerous teaching. Useless to cry over a strange little boy? So be it. But why cry over one's brother?"[74] Beauvoir goes on to use the incident to discuss Camus' "stranger," the man in the novel of the same name who feels disconnected to everything. According to Beauvoir, the stranger's mistake is to not know that connections are made by our *acts*; we are not born into them. The ability to know this is part of the definition of the self that Beauvoir uses: "subjectivity is not inert . . . [but is] a movement toward the other . . . [in which] the difference between the other and myself is abolished. . . . 'This little boy *is* not my brother.' But if I cry over him, he is no longer a stranger. It is my tears that decide."[75] Beauvoir uses these three passages on the death of Louise's baby in her writings to present a number of issues related to the existential self. First is the connection between the self and others that is the hallmark of her existentialism. This connection can be traced from its negative appearance in her first published work, *She Came to Stay*, with the epigraph from Hegel: "Each consciousness seeks the death of the other," to her third work, *The Blood of Others*, which begins with a very different epigraph from Dostoyevsky: "Each of us is responsible for everything and to every human being." Beauvoir blends this notion of the self with the economic issue of the oppression of the working class in *Memoirs* ("existence here was a slow death") and *The Blood of Others*. In *Pyrrhus et Cinéas* Beauvoir stresses injustice, yet she does not focus on the economic oppression of the working class by the bourgeoisie. Rather she emphasizes how separation from others is carried by the notion of familial membership, a sort of property designation, since the parents' insistence, "this little boy isn't your brother," is in their eyes a reason for not being connected, for not caring—but this is "a dangerous teaching."[76]

The second passage on death is part of an extended discussion on Simone's spirituality, ending with her atheism, at about the age of twelve. Simone became aware of her separateness and aloneness, and aware of the inevitability of her own death. Alone one day in the family's apartment in Paris, she became horrified at the prospect of her death: "I realized that I was condemned to death. . . . I screamed and tore at the red carpet. . . . It seemed to me impossible that I could live all through life with such horror. . . . Even more than death itself I feared that terror that would soon be with me always."[77] However, this awareness of death, with the terror that accompanied it, became a springboard to her project of a writing career; "as soon as I had given up all hopes of heaven, my worldly ambitions increased; I had to get on in life," she says.[78] This included rejecting motherhood as well; the life of the scholar and writer seemed to her to contain a purpose which a mother's life did not. When Zaza made comparisons between creating babies and creating books, she found them unacceptable:

I couldn't see any common denominator between these two modes of existence. To have children, who in their turn would have more children, was simply to go on playing the same old tune *ad infinitum*; the scholar, the artist, the writer, and the thinker created other worlds, all sweetness and light, in which everything had purpose. That was where I wished to spend my life.[79]

PITY FOR GIRLS

Throughout Beauvoir's autobiographies, the existential self meets the gendered self. Her sense of herself as exceptional, a unique subject in the existential sense, is accompanied by her denial of any negative effects of genderization on herself, not only in *Memoirs* but in the other works as well. Though she denies this, discussions of gender are present. In *Memoirs* she obliquely acknowledges a gendered self by her specific denial that she had any awareness that being a girl, a female self, made any difference to her growing up. Though she acknowledges that her "feminine condition" existed, she denies any consciousness of it: "I had no brother; there were no comparisons to make which would have revealed to me that certain liberties were not permitted me on the grounds of my sex; I attributed the restraints that were put upon me to my age. Being a child filled me with a passionate resentment; my feminine gender, never."[80] Yet she tells us that she was becoming more and more docile, in spite of her original independent spirit, so that by the age of eight, she was "a well-behaved little girl." (Since Beauvoir repeats part of the title here, "*une petite fille rangée*," her translator should have expressed the repetition, making "*rangée*" "dutiful" here, instead of "well-behaved.")[81]

But Beauvoir had already noted that her sister's gender, as well as her own, was a disappointment to her parents, though for significantly different reasons: "Her birth had been a disappointment, because the whole family had been hoping for a boy; certainly no one ever held it against her for being a girl, but it is perhaps not altogether without significance that her cradle was the centre of regretful comment."[82] In spite of the disappointment, Beauvoir maintains that there was no bitterness toward Poupette. In Poupette's case, the disappointment in her gender had nothing to do with her self as a specific person, since it was the result of having been born a second girl in a family which wanted a boy and had no boys. In Simone's case, however, the fact that she was not a boy was a disappointment because she was so bright and her gender limited her:

"What a pity Simone wasn't a boy; she could have gone to the Polytechnique!" I had often heard my parents giving vent to this complaint. A student at the Military Academy . . . was already "someone." But my sex debarred them from entertaining such lofty ambitions for me . . . I made things worse for myself by expressing a desire to become a teacher: . . . [My father] made . . . serious charges against schoolteachers; they belonged to the dangerous sect that had stood in defence of Dreyfus: the intellectuals.[83]

When she quotes her parents' continual complaint, "what a pity Simone wasn't a boy," she presents the reader with more than an acknowledgment of the parents' understanding and acceptance of patriarchy. Beauvoir quotes this in the same autobiographical work, *Memoirs*, in which she specifically *denies* that she had any awareness that being a girl had made any difference to her growing up. Thus she obliquely acknowledges a gendered self in two ways: first, by her specific denial that being a girl made any difference; and second, by later quoting her parents' disappointments, for her and for Poupette. The remarks had enough effect that they were remembered and selected for inclusion in an autobiographical work relating her first eighteen years; they were, literally, "remarkable" words. In a sense, Simone herself was the brother she didn't have, for her parents' comparisons were made not to a real brother, a male other, but to her self in an ideal form—that is, as a male, in that they saw it as tragic that she was flawed: "What a pity Simone wasn't a boy," they said.[84]

Embedded in her self gendered as feminine (as perhaps it is in all women) was a feminist self. Even in so well-brought up a self as this one, there were significant rebellions against the creation of her feminine self. An example arises in the description of the type of doll play in which she and her sister engaged, when they assumed the roles of mothers without fathers: their husbands were always "away." This early in her life, the domestic feminine condition seemed so odious to Simone (even in the bourgeois household in which she was raised, where there was often domestic help) that in formulating her own future, she decided she would have no children.[85]   This anti-marriage-and-motherhood attitude continued far beyond the time of doll play.[86]

She later also had a conscious sense of the sexism inherent in the double moral standard and had a strong reaction to it; "despite public opinion, I persisted in my view that both sexes should observe the same rules of chastity and obedience," she tells us.[87] Along with and in spite of this sense of basic fairness, Beauvoir had for many years an attitude of strong ambivalence toward her own gender. This is best perceived in some remarks made much later in *Memoirs*.   As a brilliant young university student befriended by the best male students (a list which included Merleau-Ponty, Levi-Strauss, Jean Hyppolite, as well as Sartre), she says she never regretted being a woman. Her acceptance of the common belief that the female sex was intellectually inferior to men made her own intellectual success all the more satisfying, since it meant she was an exception to her gender; "far from envying [men], I felt that my own position . . . was one of privilege . . . [yet] I did not renounce my femininity," she says.[88]

In some places, the notion of the One and Only Sovereign Self that Beauvoir uses in *Memoirs* is closer to essentialism than existentialism. Though she implies that the self is an individual, the freedom that this self desires is positive, not the negative freedom of the existential self. In later chapters, I will show that when Beauvoir experienced her earliest "romantic" relationships, those with her friend Zaza and with Sartre, her sense of self disappeared. The great contrast this made with her earlier One and Only Sovereign Self threatened her; for Beauvoir, such a change of status could only be righted by the authorial voice and authority that autobiographical writing provided.

NOTES

1. Richard N. Coe, *When the Grass Was Taller* (New Haven, CT: Yale University Press, 1984), p. xi.

2. Coe, p. 288.

3. Coe, p. 288.

4. Coe, p. 202. Coe follows this remark with a quotation from James Kirkup, the translator of Beauvoir's *Memoirs*. Kirkup wrote an autobiography that Coe highly respects, one of a group that he calls "poetic autobiographies" (which also includes *Memoirs*). It is surprising that Coe uses Kirkup here, since one would assume that, as translator of a major work by a major French existentialist, Kirkup would have had a more than average interest in, and perhaps sensitivity to, the issues that existentialist philosophy raised. Kirkup's autobiography, *The Only Child*, was published in 1957, a year before *Memoirs*, and two years before his translation of it appeared.

5. Coe, p. 203.

6. Simone de Beauvoir, *Memoirs of a Dutiful Daughter*, trans. James Kirkup (New York: Harper Colophon Books, 1974), pp. 14–7. (Hereafter, *Memoirs*.)

7. *Memoirs*, p. 16.

8. *Memoirs*, p. 16.

9. *Memoirs*, p. 17.

10. *Memoirs*, p. 18. Neither the date of these events nor her age is specified, in keeping with her common but not consistent practice in the autobiographies. We can assume that these incidents took place around or before October 1913, when she was five and a half years old, since she provides this date on page 21 of *Memoirs;* it marked the beginning of her formal schooling.

11. *Memoirs*, p. 18.

12. *Memoirs*, p. 15.

13. *Memoirs*, p. 19.

14. *Memoirs*, p. 17.

15. *Memoirs*, p. 17.

16. *Memoirs*, p. 17.

17. Simone de Beauvoir, *The Prime of Life*, trans. Peter Green (Cleveland: World Publishing Company/Meridian Books, 1966), p. 119. (Hereafter, *Prime*.)

18. Simone de Beauvoir, *The Second Sex*, trans. H. M. Parshley (New York: Vintage, 1989), p. 710.

19. *Prime*, p. 135.

20. *The Second Sex*, p. xx.

21. *Memoirs*, p. 17.

22. Simone de Beauvoir, *La Force de l'âge* (Paris: Gallimard, 1960), p. 215. *Prime*, p. 167.

23. *Memoirs*, pp. 14–5.

24. Simone de Beauvoir, *The Ethics of Ambiguity*, trans. Bernard Frechtman (New York: Citadel Press, 1970), p. 36. (Hereafter, *Ethics*.)

25. This doesn't appear in the English translation, and is really a summary of the Pythagorean position, rather than a direct quotation from Pythagoras.

26. Simone de Beauvoir, *Le Deuxième sexe* (Paris: Gallimard, 1949), unnumbered page at beginning of book.

27. *Memoirs*, p. 51.

28. *Memoirs*, p. 127.

29. *Memoirs*, pp. 128–9.

30. *Memoirs*, p. 51.

31. *Memoirs*, pp. 51–2.

32. *Memoirs*, p. 52.

33. *Memoirs*, pp.186–7.

34. *Memoirs*, p.187.

35. *Ethics*, p. 40.

36. *Memoirs*, p. 108. Note my emphasis; the English is misleading here on the issue of the self. The French has *la vérité de mon être* for which the translator chose "my essential self" and *ma vérité*, for which he chose "the self." See Simone de Beauvoir, *Mémoires d'une jeune fille rangée* (Paris: Gallimard, 1958), p. 110.

37. *Memoirs*, p. 110.

38. *Memoirs*, p. 111.

39. *Memoirs*, p. 127.

40. Herbert Marcuse, *One-Dimensional Man* (Boston: Beacon Press, 1964), p. 84.

41. *Memoirs*, pp. 190–1.

42. These phrases appear on p. 192 in *each* edition, French and English.

43. *Memoirs*, p. 193. Because she reverts to classification and cataloguing in *All Said and Done*, one might indeed wonder whether she had returned to the ways of her parents.

44. *Memoirs*, pp. 11–2.

45. *Memoirs*, pp. 30–1.

46. *Memoirs*, p. 12.

47. *Memoirs*, p. 17.

48. Beauvoir states this both in *Memoirs*, p. 360, and in *Prime*, p. 285. Later, in *Force of Circumstance*, trans. Richard Howard (New York: Harper Colophon Books, 1977), p. 649, she criticized those women who had read *Memoirs* because they liked her description of an upbringing they shared, yet were uninterested in her later explanations of how she had escaped it (i.e., specifically the story of her writing career).

49. Beauvoir uses the pseudonym "Mabille" for Zaza's surname in her writings. Translator James Kirkup changes the French spelling, "Elisabeth," to "Elizabeth." See Kate and Edward Fullbrook, *Simone de Beauvoir and Jean-Paul Sartre: The Remaking of a Twentieth-Century Legend* (New York: HarperCollins, 1994).

50. *Memoirs*, p. 360.

51. *Prime*, p. 9.

52. *Prime*, p. 9.

53. *Ethics*, p. 119.

54. *Force*, pp. 66–8. She says here that she was most irritated by this book, of all the books she wrote, particularly by its idealism: "I was in error when I thought I could define a morality independent of a social context. I could write an historical novel without having a philosophy of history, but not construct a theory of action. . . . Why did I write *concrete liberty* instead of *bread*?"

55. *Ethics*, p. 25.

56. *Ethics*, p. 156.

57. Sartre's *Being and Nothingness* is subtitled: *A Phenomenological Essay on Ontology*.

58. *Memoirs*, p. 360.

59. *Memoirs*, p. 282.

60. On the identity of "Pradelle," see Terry Keefe, *Simone de Beauvoir: A Study of Her Writings* (Totowa, NJ: Barnes and Noble Books, 1983), p. 13; and also Claude Francis and Fernande Gontier, *Simone de Beauvoir: a Life . . . a Love Story*, trans. Lisa Nesselson (New York: St. Martin's Press, 1987), p. 63. This amazing and sad story seems now, finally, to be completely told.

61. *Memoirs*, p. 360.

62. *Ethics*, p. 73.

63. I'm grateful to Neil Hertz for this idea.

64. *Memoirs*, pp. 5 and 42.

65. *Memoirs*, pp. 42 and 45.

66. *Memoirs*, p. 42.

67. *Memoirs*, p. 43.

68. *Memoirs*, p. 45.

69. *Memoirs*, p. 45.

70. *Memoirs*, p. 131.

71. *Memoirs*, p. 131.

72. Simone de Beauvoir, *The Blood of Others*, trans. Roger Senhouse and Yvonne Moyse (New York: Pantheon, 1983) pp. 7–8.

73. *The Blood of Others*, p. 10.

74. Simone de Beauvoir, *Pyrrhus et Cinéas* (Paris: Gallimard, 1944), p. 13. (Hereafter, *PC*.)

75. *PC*, pp. 16–7.

76. *PC*, p. 13.

77. *Memoirs*, p. 138. Beauvoir's "preoccupation" with death—in novels, as well as elsewhere—has been discussed by others. An early book by Elaine Marks, *Simone de Beauvoir: Encounters with Death* (New Brunswick, NJ: Rutgers University Press, 1973), covers some of the territory, though Marks is unsympathetic and, I think, ultimately unfair to Beauvoir in this book. Marks is also not careful enough about the philosophical issues with which Beauvoir was grappling. Beauvoir discusses her own feelings toward death in the greatest detail at the end of *Prime*, pp. 474–9. I don't think that Beauvoir discusses death to any extent that should be considered unusual for someone who was writing existentialist philosophy and novels, as well as an autobiography.

78. *Memoirs*, p. 141.

79. *Memoirs*, pp. 140–1.

80. *Memoirs*, p. 55.

81. *Memoirs*, p. 61. *Mémoires*, p. 63.

82. *Memoirs*, p. 42.

83. *Memoirs*, pp. 177–8.

84. *Memoirs*, p. 177.

85. *Memoirs*, p. 56.

86. *Memoirs*, p. 87 and *Prime*, p. 34.
87. *Memoirs*, pp. 166–7.
88. *Memoirs*, p. 295.

5

Writing the Self: The Woman in Love

For Simone, the chinks in the armor of the free and sovereign self began with her first passionate love, the worshipful adolescent love she had for her friend Zaza, whom she met at school when both were about ten years old. In Beauvoir's autobiography, Zaza enters and exits in tragic stories, and both tragedies leave a strong impression on Simone. The last, Zaza's death, is used by Beauvoir as the end-frame of her own life story in *Memoirs*.

BELOVED FRIEND, ALTER EGO

Before she began her schooling, Zaza had been burned—seriously enough that it had taken her a year to recuperate. In Beauvoir's eyes, that accident became a symbol of Zaza's uniqueness; "Nothing as important as that had ever happened to me; she at once seemed to me a very finished person," Beauvoir says.[1] In addition to the importance lent her by her accident, Zaza had poise, a sophistication in speaking, and an impishness that added to Simone's admiration of her. Beauvoir tells us, referring to those first few days of knowing Zaza, "Her conquest of me was complete . . . everything she had to say was either interesting or amusing."[2]

Zaza also exhibited remarkable personal freedom. More prone to engage in conventional behavior, but attracted to spontaneity, Simone greatly admired this. "I was completely won over by Zaza's vivacity and independence of spirit," she tells us.[3] So, though Simone and Zaza were closely matched intellectually, in Simone's eyes, Zaza was the stronger, more mature person: "She was said to have 'personality': that was her supreme advantage. . . . 'I've no personality,' I would sadly tell myself. . . . I loved Zaza so much that she seemed to be more real than myself;

I was her negative (*d'ordinaire avant elle*)."[4] Simone knew that Zaza was important to her, though it took a while before she realized how strong her feelings were for her. Beauvoir's openness in describing this makes it easy for the reader to see connections between this early love and the later love she had for Sartre. When she saw Zaza again after the first summer vacation following the year they met, she was shocked into an awareness of her passionate connection to Zaza. As she describes this, it was akin to an evangelical conversion:

my tongue was suddenly loosened, and a thousand bright suns began blazing in my breast; radiant with happiness, I told myself: "That's what was wrong; I needed Zaza!" . . . This was a blinding revelation. All at once, conventions, routines, and the careful categorizing of emotions were swept away and I was overwhelmed by a flood of feeling that had no place in any code. . . . a wave of joy . . . as violent and fresh as a waterfalling cataract (*l'eau des cascades*), as naked, beautiful, and bare as a granite cliff.[5]

Accompanying this description of the realization of her intense love for Zaza is a recollection of her girlhood fear of Zaza's death (an eerie recollection, since by the time Beauvoir had written this autobiography, Zaza was dead). On a day when Zaza was absent from school, Simone was chilled and "comforted" at the same time to realize her dependence on her:

[I wondered] "what if she were to die, then what would happen to me?" It was rather frightening . . . all my happiness, my very existence, lay in her hands. . . . Well, if that were to happen, I told myself, I should die on the spot. . . . This rationalization gave me comfort. . . . I had gone as far as to admit the extent of [my] dependence . . . I did not dare envisage all its consequences.[6]

What these consequences might be was left unstated, but Beauvoir probably meant to direct the reader's thoughts to the possibility of a physical love affair between them, for the relationship had "an intensity which could not be accounted for by any established set of rules and conventions," she says.[7]

Beauvoir recounts a story she read at the age of thirteen which made a strong impression on her because it seemed that the two same-sex characters, Theagenus and Euphorion, were much like herself and Zaza:

Theagenus, an earnest, painstaking, and sensible schoolboy, was captivated by good-looking Euphorion; this young aristocrat . . . artistic, witty, and impertinent, dazzled his schoolfellows and teachers, though he was often reproached for his easy-going ways. *He died in the flower of his youth, and it was Theagenus who fifty years later told their story.* I identified Zaza with the handsome blond . . . myself with Theagenus . . . there were obviously people who were gifted and people who were merely talented, and I classed myself irremediably in the latter category. [8] [italics added]

When Beauvoir wrote this at the age of fifty, Zaza was dead, also "in the flower of her youth," and Beauvoir was alive and telling the tale. In identifying with the story (André Laurie's *Schoolboy in Athens*), Simone understands that, as the "merely talented" one, she was in a sense inferior; in another sense, she—the *writer*—was superior: "in the end it was Theagenus who survived his friend and wrote about him: he was *both mind and memory, the essential Subject* [italics added]. If it had been suggested that I should be Zaza, I should have refused; I preferred owning the universe to having a single face."[9]

Her deep friendship with Zaza continued into high school and her beginning years of college ("Zaza was still my only real friend," she says at one point),[10] but also states that she was growing apart from her: "I no longer preferred her above all others."[11] As Simone grew emotionally independent of her family and the bourgeois culture of which they were a part, and as she increasingly felt and used her own freedom, a new contrast between the two young women appeared. Simone understood that Zaza, though an intelligent person and successful student, was not taking the same path she was; because of family pressures and what had become her own inclinations by now, she was too firmly tied to her family and willing to carry out its desires for her. Zaza's mother increased her demands and her tyranny. She refused to permit Zaza to earn a degree, afraid she would become an intellectual, and—in a class where marriages were still arranged—marital love was unlikely.[12] Simone felt a growing ambivalence to Zaza; though she ends Book Three of *Memoirs* by asserting that they still agreed on most things, she also notes important differences between them.[13] For example, in a letter to Simone, Zaza had exhibited a sacrificial side of herself in passages like the following, which alarmed Simone: "the renunciation of self, of existence, of everything; the renunciation made by those who try to begin the life of the hereafter here on earth—if you only knew how much it tempts me. . . . I could never go whole-heartedly for life as you do."[14] Clearly, the growing contrast between the two friends was something Zaza perceived, as well as Simone, when in regard to Zaza's remark about having a religious vocation, Beauvoir comments, "if ever she entered a convent she would be lost to me; and to herself, I thought."[15]

As Simone realized the increasing threat to Zaza, she became determined to fight "to prevent her life becoming a living death."[16] This marks the ending of Book Three of *Memoirs*, and it is echoed at the end of *Memoirs*, summarizing Beauvoir's sense of failure and guilt at Zaza's death: "We had fought together against the revolting fate that had lain ahead of us, and for a long time I believed that I had paid for my own freedom with her death."[17] Because these two lives paralleled each other for so long, the one who moved into "freedom," who survived to define a self apart from an existence as a dutiful daughter, felt guilty for her own success. Since she had "decided to fight with all [her] strength" so that Zaza would live a freer life, and had made herself responsible for Zaza, it seemed that when Zaza died of "complications" of her life and her position, Simone had failed in the task she set herself: to help Zaza.

In her last autobiography, *All Said and Done*, Beauvoir summarizes this childhood friendship with Zaza. The summary comes in the book's first chapter, in a passage where she discusses friends and lovers, within a quasi-philosophcal discussion of "chance" (*hasard*).[18] In her summary of the love-friendship with Zaza, she repeats the catalogue of those qualities that attracted Simone to Zaza: her independent spirit, her vivacity, her intelligence. In comparing Zaza to Poupette, Beauvoir found her sister "less extremely eager for knowledge" than she was, while Zaza was "lively and intelligent."[19] So she and Zaza, both bright, were coupled intellectually as she and Sartre were later, and as she and Poupette were not. The strength of the attractiveness of these qualities created an intimacy; "through Zaza I came to know the joy of loving, the delight of intellectual exchange and of daily intimate alliance. She made me give up my role of the good little girl; and she taught me independence and disrespect," she says.[20] The intimacy between herself and Poupette was beneficial to Simone too, but in a very different way. In *All Said and Done*, Beauvoir says of Poupette: "I should count the fact of having had a sister, younger than myself but close to me in age, as one of my pieces of good luck. She helped me to assert myself. I invented the mixture of authority and affection that marked my dealings with her."[21] Unlike her relationship with Poupette, the relationship with Zaza, one of passionate love, developed Simone's appreciation for independence, because independence was one of Zaza's qualities. As in her relationship with Sartre, passionate love emerged for Simone when she was looking up to someone, when the lover was seen as a superior in some ways, not an equal nor an inferior.

As time went on, the pupil began to surpass the teacher, for much of this "independence and disrespect" was inaccessible to Zaza herself, at least in regard to her family. She was sincere in her filial devotion and her piety, and continued to be, unto death; while Simone grew more rebellious toward her family and her class. It was tragic that Zaza's relationship with Maurice Merleau-Ponty was forbidden by her family, for specific reasons they felt could not be overlooked. Yet there had been another relationship, and another break forced by her family, with André, another young man she had loved.[22] (Merleau-Ponty was not the only imperfect mate for Zaza, it seems.) Loyalty was owed to her family, whatever the cost to herself. One can read a certain irony into the title, *Memoirs of a Dutiful Daughter*, since Simone, the autobiographer, became the "undutiful daughter." Zaza, continuing to be the "dutiful daughter," was unable to survive into adulthood adhering to the interdictions of her family about her love life. As it progresses, *Memoirs* becomes a memoir of two young women, two intimate friends: the dutiful (soon-to-be-dead) daughter, Zaza, and the undutiful but alive daughter, Simone. Because of Zaza's tragic flaw and Simone's changing values, the tables turned; Zaza became the "negative" and Simone the "positive," until finally Zaza/Euphorion became the corpse, and Simone/Theagenus the chronicler of her death.

Memoirs leaves us with Beauvoir's existentialist and feminist message that a necessary part of survival is independence, an independence forged from concrete choices one makes in regard to the details of life: "I made a decision. . . . I would leave home; I would take a place of my own . . . I would earn my own living and be free to come and go, to have people in and to write: life was really beginning to open out."[23] The story *Memoirs* tells is of one "woman in love" who is destroyed, unable to progress from being a dutiful daughter to a woman independent of her family's attempts to control her future and define her self; and another, Simone, who makes the break, escapes family pressures to control and define her, who survives, and not only survives, but flourishes. But she too had her own problems as a "woman in love."

During Simone's adolescence and early adulthood, she carried on a somewhat obligatory and lackluster romance with her cousin, Jacques. Though Zaza remained the center of her emotional life, Jacques played the part of the token man, a necessary love interest to a young woman of her class, since he provided at least a possibility of marriage. Yet Beauvoir tells us that the prospect of marriage with Jacques seemed to be potentially more restrictive than liberating:

For Jacques, *marriage* was obviously an end in itself, and I didn't want to put *an end to anything*, at least not so soon. . . . At moments I was able to persuade myself that I could live alongside Jacques without mutilating myself and then terror would seize me again: "What? Imprison myself in the limitations of another human being? . . . Not yet; I'm not ready: I don't want to sacrifice *myself*, the whole of *myself*."[24] [italics added]

In the contrast between this passage and the previous one ("life was really beginning to open out"), Beauvoir defines the problem she faced, as do many women: traditional marriage comes at the cost of imprisonment of the self.

In the last pages of *Memoirs*, Beauvoir chronicles two tragedies, and both were about former loves of hers. Though the death of Zaza ends the book, prior to that we learn the rest of Jacques' story: he married someone who eventually detested him; his womanizing and drinking caused the marriage to end. Eventually a complete alcoholic, he died of malnutrition at the age of forty-six.[25] The last time she saw him, a year before he died, he cried, "Oh! Why didn't I marry *you*!"[26] (One reason was that his mother had advised him against marrying her, since they were cousins.)

Thus, in her late teens and early adulthood, Simone as "the woman in love" was caught up in a drama composed of several issues and characters: first, her continuing love for Zaza, no longer as intense as it had been, yet now carrying with it a responsibility for Zaza's welfare; second, her romance with her cousin, Jacques, a person who provided a necessary romantic interest for her, but whose ideas on marriage were not to Simone's liking; and third, her new love for Sartre and her inclusion in his intellectual clique.

"THE DREAM-COMPANION . . . THE DOUBLE"

After she met Sartre, she officially ended the ambiguous relationship with Jacques. What she had found was a companion, but even more, a way to live out the future she desired for herself:

the future suddenly seemed . . . more difficult than I had reckoned but . . . more certain; instead of undefined possibilities I saw opening out before me a clearly-marked field of activity . . . I no longer asked myself: what shall I do? There was everything to be done, *everything I had formerly longed to do*: to combat error, to find the truth, to tell it and expound it to the world, perhaps to help to change the world. . . . everything was possible.[27] [italics added]

It was not just because she had met Sartre that "everything was possible." She had begun to realize she had a future, because she took control of it, lived out her choices, and became an undutiful daughter.

Meeting Sartre also made her reassess herself in certain ways. While it made her a clearer thinker, it also gave her a dose of intellectual humility (and perhaps a sense of inferiority); for the first time in her life, she felt that she was intellectually inferior to someone; "after so many years of arrogant solitude, it was something serious to discover that I wasn't the One and Only, but one among many, by no means first, and suddenly uncertain of my true capacity," she tells us.[28] At the end of *Force of Circumstance*, Beauvoir reflected again on Sartre's importance to her life. She voiced the concerns of the existential self for freedom, and for the ability to create one's self through choosing one's future: "I could only have become attached to a man who was hostile to all that I loathed: the Right, conventional thinking, religion. It was no matter of chance that I chose Sartre; for after all I did choose him. I followed him joyfully because he led me along the paths I wanted to take."[29] The autobiographical admission of her "secondariness" ("I followed him joyfully") probably did not quiet her critics, convinced for years of her intellectual dependence on Sartre, nor did it please her defenders. In it, one hears echoes of her earlier remarks about Zaza, the "gifted one," and Simone, the "merely talented one."

Yet, though she acknowledged Sartre's lead in certain ways, she insisted on distinguishing this from the production of her own ideas and writings. In this, she voices the concern of the gendered woman-self:

It has been said by some people that Sartre writes my books. . . . Long before I came on the scene they were saying that Colette "slept her way" to fame; so anxious is our society to maintain the accepted status of members of my sex as secondary beings, reflections, toys or parasites of the all-important male. Even more strongly held is the belief that all my convictions were put into my head by Sartre.[30]

In these attacks, she recognized a familiar form of sexism, one she had often heard growing up: "Fifty years have gone by, but this is still the same old idea my father held: 'A woman is what her husband makes her' . . . people in our society really do believe that a woman thinks with her uterus—what low-mindedness, really!"[31] Along with the intellectual secondariness that the relationship with Sartre created came a strong companionship, life with a mate with whom, unlike those other men, it was easy to communicate: "the dream-companion I had longed for since I was fifteen . . . the double."[32] So, to replace Zaza ("we were the two inseparables"),[33] who in a sense was a replacement for Poupette ("she was my alter-ego, my double"), she had found another double. This time her double turned out to be a male:

Until then, the men I had been fond of . . . were of a different order from my own . . . it was impossible to communicate with them without reserves. Sartre corresponded exactly to the dream-companion I had longed for since I was fifteen: he was the double in whom I found all my burning aspiration raised to the pitch of incandescence. I should always be able to share everything with him. . . . I knew that he would never go out of my life again.[34]

A RELATIVE BEING, AN OTHER

In *The Prime of Life*, when Beauvoir narrates the story of the early years of her relationship with Sartre, she insists on feeling she had an exceptional status, beyond the bonds of womanhood. "Just as previously I had refused to be labeled a 'child,' so now I did not think of myself as a 'woman.' I was *me*."[35] This comparison, that the child is to the self as the woman is to the self, is striking. Beauvoir refused the application of categorization to herself in both cases, sensing that such a categorization was a condemnation to limitations and a secondary status. In her autobiographies, as well as in some interviews, Beauvoir repeatedly attempted either to exclude herself from gender categorizations or acknowledged that, in earlier days though no longer, she did so.

However, in the case of Beauvoir as woman (as in the earlier one, Simone as child), she was condemned to a form of categorization anyway. In the terms she used in *The Second Sex*, the story she tells of the early years she and Sartre spent together show that Simone's "femininity" (the genderization of women) may have intensified in the relationship with Sartre, and that, as a "woman in love," she was becoming more of a "relative being."

In *The Prime of Life*, Beauvoir presents Simone, then in her mid-twenties, as confused and besieged, in fact even "bewitched," in regard to her own identity. Not her self, but Sartre, the other, the "double," took center stage in her existence. What followed was concern, anxiety, in fact, fear: "During my subjugation by Zaza I plumbed the black depths of humility; now the same story was repeated, except that I fell from a greater height, and my self-confidence had been more rudely shaken . . . so fascinated was I by the other person that I forgot myself, so much so indeed that no part of me remained to register the statement: *I am nothing*."[36] This is not a statement of the type of existential conversion described by Heidegger, Sartre, and Beauvoir herself in *The Ethics of Ambiguity*. Rather, it should be interpreted as an example of the passionate person, a type described in *Ethics*, and as an example of the woman in love, a type described in *The Second Sex*. Beauvoir had said in *Ethics* that in "maniacal" passion, freedom is not genuine because the passionate person seeks possession of the object, an impossibility: "having involved his whole life with an external object which can continually escape him, he tragically feels his dependence. Even if it does not definitely disappear, the object never gives itself."[37] The passionate person achieves the sort of negativity that focuses on her/his own subjectivity, not on the world, says Beauvoir: "[he] makes himself a lack of being not that there might *be* being, but in order to be. And he remains at a distance; he is never fulfilled."[38] The result is an intense sense of emptiness, since the self has been so closely connected with the existence of the other, but of the other as object, not as freedom: "one . . . considers the solitude in which this subjectivity encloses itself as injurious. Having withdrawn into an unusual region of the world, seeking not to communicate with other men, this freedom is realized only as a separation."[39]

Françoise, the protagonist of *She Came to Stay* (the "Beauvoir" character in this *roman à clef*), experiences herself as "nothing" but a nothing that is so intense that there is no one left to say, "I am nothing." This occurs at the moment in the novel when she is separated from the other two people in the romantic "trio." Beauvoir presents these thoughts on her gendered self as a woman in love in the process of making an analysis of this, her first published work, insisting that her personal experience underlies the work. While in other places she insists that certain works were not *romans à clef*, she insists that this *was;* it was the working out of a painful personal experience, the *ménage à trois* of herself, former student Olga Kosakievicz, and Sartre. The affair was based on a philosophical distinction which the twenty-three year old Sartre had made—with which Beauvoir supposedly agreed: "He explained the matter to me in his favorite terminology. 'What *we* have,' he said, 'is an *essential* love; but it is a good idea for us also to experience *contingent* love affairs.' We were two of a kind, and our relationship would endure as long as we did; but it could not make up entirely for the fleeting riches to be had from encounters with different people."[40] An extraordinary passage describes the manner in which she wrote *She Came to Stay*. Beauvoir makes direct comparisons between the self-conceptions of herself and Françoise, the main character of the novel:

I endowed [Françoise] with my own experiences. . . . She regarded herself as conscious mind . . . the only such in existence; she had allowed Pierre to share her sovereign position . . . But there was a price to pay for this . . . by merging her identity with everything she was she lost all sharply defined individualism in her own eyes. I had become aware of this shortcoming earlier, when I made comparisons between myself and Zaza . . . [Françoise] told herself . . . that she was nobody, nobody at all. . . . she tried to draw on her own inner resources for support—but in vain. She had, literally, no real self (*moi*).[41]

In this passage, Beauvoir compares the earlier intense relationship she had with Zaza with the relationship with Sartre. Once again, she coupled with someone she considered superior to herself, and, for a time, the result was disastrous for her; she became the "negative" to the "positive," a merely relative being, like the Other she described in *The Second Sex*. Once again, as in relating her and Zaza's story in *Memoirs*, she used her writing, her authorship, to establish some authority for her self. Through the creation of the character of Françoise, Beauvoir acknowledged a shift that took place in her own sense of her self with the onset of passionate love:

She was an utterly transparent creature, without features or individuality. When she let herself slip into the clinging hell of passion, there was one thing which consoled her for her fall from grace: her very limitations and vulnerability made a human being of her, with precisely mapped contours . . . from a position of absolute and all-embracing authority she was suddenly reduced to an infinitely tiny particle in the external universe.[42]

Here, Beauvoir describes a moment of awareness that arises from the experience of a woman in love. She had attempted an impossibility, one Beauvoir had analyzed in *The Second Sex* in the chapter, "The Woman in Love." There, she says that the woman in love is similar to the mystic in her wish to lose herself in the being of the other: "the childhood dream, the mystic dream, the dream of love: to attain supreme existence through losing oneself in the other."[43]

KILLING THE OTHER

But this awareness was different from her earlier one concerning Zaza. Now there was not one, but *two* others: the original love, Sartre, and the other woman, Olga. The other woman constituted a double threat; first, she was a threat to the individual (Simone/Françoise), because of her demanding personality: "Now another danger threatened her, one which I myself had been endeavoring to exorcise ever since my adolescence. Other people (*autrui*) could not only steal the world from her, but also invade her personality and bewitch her. Xavière, with her outbursts of temper . . . was disfiguring Françoise's inner self."[44] With premonitions of this danger, Beauvoir already had taken steps to avoid it. Earlier in the autobiography, when discussing the relationship she and Sartre had with her former student, Olga, she had said: "I . . . determined not to allow Olga too important a place in my life. . . . Nor had I any intention of yielding up to her the sovereign position that *I* had always occupied, in the very center of the universe. Little by little, however, I began to compromise: my need to agree with Sartre on all subjects outweighed the desire to see Olga through eyes other than his."[45] The other woman became a threat to the original couple. She was a threat to an individual who had become a "we," and whose self had become a "negative" to the "positive" (Sartre/Pierre). In this case, however, the act of agreement necessary to maintain the "we" (Simone's "need to agree with Sartre on all subjects") was the same act that threatened the "we" and that, therefore, threatened her self, her "companionate self," at this point in her life. Without the "trio," no agreement with Sartre; without agreement with Sartre, no (companionate) self and no couple. In this case, three equaled two. The only solution to Beauvoir's dilemma was "the final solution." The novel's murderous finale is defended in the following passage in which Beauvoir explains why she decided to "kill" Olga through the character, Xavière:

by killing Olga on paper I purged every twinge of irritation and resentment I had previously felt toward her, and cleansed our friendship of all the unpleasant memories that lurked among those of a happier nature . . . the process of self-iden-tification came off. . . . when I wrote [the final pages] my throat was as tight as though I had the burden of a real murder on my shoulders.[46]

Through this "on-paper killing" of Olga, Beauvoir purged her self of both threats presented by the other woman. Because love brought "the fall," in which "from a position of absolute and all-embracing authority she was suddenly reduced to an infinitely tiny particle in the external universe,"[47] it required a reestablishment of authority through authorship: first, through the writing of a *roman à clef*, in which the other woman is sacrificed to the needs of the companionate self; and second, through the writing of autobiographies, in which the stories of the past self and its important others are managed by the authority of the author.

We can compare this to her other act, the writing of the death of Zaza, as narrated by the autobiographical self of Beauvoir. It was only when she self-consciously became the authorial overseer in her own drama, either in autobiography per se or in a *roman à clef*, that she released herself from the hurt caused by the disasters that she had encountered in her own life.

THE COMPANIONATE SELF

Whether there was any "irritation and resentment" at Sartre (as there was at Olga), and whether that was purged and if so, how, is not addressed here by Beauvoir. It is striking that Françoise and, we assume, Beauvoir perceived the other woman as the villain. Both Olga and the character patterned on her, Xavière, are specifically mentioned as the "problem for Françoise," while Sartre/Pierre escapes being assigned the status of either a problem or a villain, even though the "trio" was his idea. At one point in *The Prime of Life* (and earlier), Beauvoir did mention that she was irritated with both Sartre and Olga, from time to time: "We had not established any real equality in our relationship with her, but had rather annexed her to ourselves. Even though I blamed Sartre on occasion, I remained firmly behind him. . . . They both continued to tell me all about their meetings. . . . At first I had welcomed these reports. . . . but . . . had come to feel an impatience I did not bother to conceal."[48] The "we" that Beauvoir formed through her relationship with Sartre, which I call "the companionate self," is one dimension of the woman in love. This notion of the self as "we," as she uses it in *The Prime of Life*, contrasts with the existentialist notion of the self as a subject marked by individual choice, responsibility, and freedom. This "we" becomes the clearest indication of the mismatch between the existential self and the gendered self. In her autobiographies after *Memoirs*, she repeatedly uses the "we" when referring to herself and Sartre, but the usage is particularly apparent in *The Prime of Life*, which is dedicated to Jean-Paul Sartre.

Many commentators have pointed out that Beauvoir's autobiographies exhibit a strong attention to Sartre and his activities. One critic has discussed Beauvoir's use of the "we" and how it relates to her self, claiming that it points to a psychic "fusion" in the couple.[49] Sartre acknowledged this extreme closeness also, but later in life. In an interview with Madeleine Gobeil, Sartre said that when someone asked a question to the two of them at the same time, one generally got the same response. He credited it to their life in common with its fund of common experiences, so that what resulted was "*une mémoire à deux.*" Adding to this *mémoire à deux*, he pointed to what might be called an *esprit et avis à deux*, and he stated flatly that he agreed with everything that she had written in her autobiography about relations between them.[50]

The repeated use of the pronoun "we" in *The Prime of Life* to indicate the couple Beauvoir-and-Sartre is a strong marker of the change in self that Beauvoir underwent at this period of her life in the direction of loss of autonomy. The self that she presents in the early part of the book is often not individualized; the "we" occurs and reoccurs in regard to an extensive variety of states, actions, and thoughts they shared—from their health and disposition, to their lack of limitations, to their emotions ("we were furious"), their expectations, their acceptances, their life choice ("we were writers"), their rejections, and their successes.[51] She continually calls attention to the similarities between herself and Sartre, for though he was her intellectual *superior*, he was also the perfect fellow traveller, since they were "marked by an identical sign."[52] She had designed a new creature, a "we," and her report is clearly cynical: "Very conveniently I persuaded myself that a foreordained harmony existed between us on every single point. 'We are,' I declared, 'as one.' This absolute certainty meant that I never went against my instinctive desires; and when, on two occasions, our desires clashed, I was completely flabbergasted."[53]

Significantly, the particular experience in which this "we" happened was that of Beauvoir's being a "woman in love." As such, she was marked by her self-surrender, by the subordination of her own existence to that of another. Beauvoir lost the autonomy with which *The Prime of Life* began, for it had begun with the excitement over her hard-won freedom—never to be disputed, never in doubt—of which she spoke in the highest existentialist terms: "I had broken free from my past, and was now self-sufficient and self-determining: I had established my autonomy once and forever, and nothing could deprive me of it."[54] For someone not content to be either a "child" or a "woman," but who insisted on being "me," one who insisted on a radical individuality, this fusion to a "we" seems like a radical change, though it isn't radical at all when seen in combination with her earlier passionate attachment to Zaza.

Beauvoir directly criticizes the "companionate self" at one point, and in regard to disagreements with Sartre, yet even there she does not greatly assert the sovereignty of the individual, as we might expect from the writer of *The Ethics of Ambiguity*. She merely allowed that *some* events are lived through individually, as in this passage written about the "trio"—Simone, Sartre, and Olga: "I was led to revise certain postulates which hitherto I had thought we were agreed upon, and told myself it was wrong to bracket myself and another person in that equivocal and all-too-handy word 'we.' There were some experiences that each individual lived through alone."[55] Because Sartre became "unbalanced" in both good and bad ways by the experience, Beauvoir felt her own emotional stability threatened, and this produced in her an "agony which . . . went far beyond mere jealousy."[56]

Within a year or two after the relationship began in earnest, Beauvoir experienced a kind of despair, losing interest in her own work, even losing her intellectual pride. The intimidation she felt due to Sartre's friends and himself was a major factor in this unproductive, "lazy" period. "You used to be full of little ideas, Beaver," Sartre said.[57] The condescending tone of this remark is intensified in the original French, a more literal translation of which is, "But before, Beaver ("*Castor*"), you thought a *lot* about *little* things."[58] In spite of her announced insistence to herself that she was her self and not a "woman," it seems that during this period she became more and more a "woman," a being whose existence is relative to a man's, as she directly compared herself to Sartre, devaluing herself. Thus we read, in her harsh summary statement of this period, the judgment: "I had ceased to exist on my own account, and was now a mere parasite."[59] This sense of parasitical existence was far removed from the autonomy she had won and celebrated by the writing of *Memoirs*, an autonomy she recalled in the preface of *The Prime of Life*: "Beneath the final line of that book an invisible question mark was inscribed, and I could not get my mind off it. Freedom I had—but freedom to do what?"[60] And again, on the first page of the book's interior: "The most intoxicating aspect of my return to Paris in September, 1929, was the freedom I now possessed. I had dreamed of it since childhood. . . . Now, suddenly, it was mine."[61]

Later in the book, we learn that she dissociated herself from philosophy, the field of her training; though still acknowledging her own philosophical critical skills and her deep interest in the field, she no longer wanted to think of herself as a philosopher:

I possessed both considerable powers of assimilation and a well-developed critical sense; and philosophy was for me a living reality, which gave me never-failing satisfaction.

Yet I did not regard myself as a philosopher . . . queries as to why I did not attempt to join the elite are surely otiose: it would be more useful to explain *how* certain individuals are capable of getting results from that conscious venture into lunacy known as a "philosophical system" from which they derive that obsessional attitude which endows their tentative patterns with universal insight and applicability. As I have remarked before, women are not by nature prone to obsessions of this type.[62]

That Beauvoir or any existentialist would write this remark is astonishing. Since it was anathema to the existentialists to claim any fixedness to human beings, her claim of natural abilities was either made ironically, or it indicates that there was an underlying disagreement in her own thinking with the tenets of existentialism (which is what I have claimed earlier).

Remarks in the autobiographies like those above cast doubt on her claim that the problem of women's condition did not directly concern her, at least not in regard to Sartre.[63] She continually maintained in *The Prime of Life* that she was never the victim of discrimination by him or his friends. In later years as well, for example, in interviews with the German journalist Alice Schwarzer, she maintained it. In response to one of Schwarzer's questions, "Given that it is very difficult to establish relationships between men and women that are based on equality, do you believe that you personally have succeeded?" she answered: "Yes, or rather, the problem never arose, because there is nothing of the oppressor about Sartre. If I'd loved someone other than Sartre, I would never have let myself be oppressed. . . . I don't think that, given the way of life we have chosen, I have often had to play the female role."[64] She had claimed that the issue of women's condition and the production of what she called "femininity" in *The Second Sex* did not arise for her as a direct analysis of her own life; it occurred through her listening to the testimony of other women. She was thirty-six years old when she discovered it:

it had not yet dawned on me that such a thing as a specifically feminine "condition" existed. Now, suddenly, I met a large number of women over forty who, in differing circumstances and with various degrees of success, had all undergone one identical experience: they had lived as "dependent persons." . . . because I was a writer . . . they told me a great deal; I began to take stock of [their] difficulties. . . . *The problem did not concern me directly* . . . but my interest had been aroused.[65] [italics added]

Thus, the issue of women's condition is presented to the reader as having come from *outside* Beauvoir, from all of those others she met who had actually felt discrimination, since she did not ever feel it (in spite of the "pity" thrown her way at not being a boy, as we saw in *Memoirs*, and the obviously limited options she felt at learning this). But in *The Prime of Life*, as she is summing up one stage of her life, she does acknowledge directly that in her own life, she too in fact had been "conditioned" into femininity, as had those others she listened to and from whom she learned about femininity. What is remarkable to her, however, is that she continually lived "freely":

I know that when certain critics read this autobiography they will point out, triumphantly, that it flatly contradicts my thesis in *The Second Sex*, a suggestion they have already made with regard to *Memoirs of a Dutiful Daughter*. . . . Have I ever claimed that I, personally, was not a woman? On the contrary, my main purpose has been to isolate and identify my own particular brand of femininity. . . . it suited me to live with a man whom I regarded as my superior . . . nothing, I believed, could impede my will. I did not deny my femininity . . . I simply ignored it.[66]

Yet, though the individual may choose to ignore it (or not acknowledge it unless it's seen as someone else's problem), discrimination of all types is more than an individual problem, and individual solutions will not be effective beyond a point.

By the end of *Force of Circumstance*, Beauvoir carefully and defensively explains her choice to follow and be overshadowed by Sartre. She made the choice, she claims, because "he led [her] along the paths [she] wanted to take," being the more suited for the role of leader, she argues, since he was the more creative thinker, both philosophically and politically. In response to the critical remarks of some feminists on her choice to follow Sartre, she neatly, if unconvincingly, insists that it was indeed a use of her freedom to acknowledge his superiority and "freely" follow him philosophically and politically (i.e., to accept his ideas). In spite of such a straightforward acknowledgment of intellectual ancestry, this raises questions.[67]

Prior to the writing of *The Second Sex*, how did she manage to live outside of the boundaries of the gendered self? In addition, how did she minimize her own contributions while acknowledging Sartre's? In what ways was she philosophically and politically creative, as she describes Sartre to be? Further, in what ways did her own thinking lead his along new paths? These last questions can be asked against Beauvoir's own protestations. Beauvoir, after all, tells us when she is being a Sartrean or when she is in agreement with his ideas. But she never (or seldom) tells us, and probably seldom noticed herself, when she was not in philosophical agreement with him. Even less often does she specifically note that she has gone beyond his thinking or initiated new ideas. For her, as for many scholars, Sartre's thinking became the lodestone.

In *Force of Circumstance*, Beauvoir describes two important affairs she had: the first was with Nelson Algren a few years after World War II; she met him on her first trip to the United States. The second was with Claude Lanzmann, which began in 1952 when she was forty-four and he was twenty-seven. In neither one of these was she "the woman in love" again, as she had been with Zaza and Sartre.

The affair with Algren is noteworthy primarily because of the degree to which he pursued her, wanting her to move to the United States and live with him, in effect, asking her to change her primary loyalty from Sartre to him, but she refused. The relationship was another proving (or disproving) ground for Sartre's theory of "essential" and "contingent" loves, as it had been for the disastrous "trio" described in *The Prime of Life*. When Beauvoir brings up the Algren affair in *Force of Circumstance*, she wants to discuss it in a very narrowly defined context: "Although I related this affair—very approximately—in *The Mandarins*, I return to it now not out of any taste for gossip, but in order to examine more closely a problem that in *The Prime of Life* I took to be too easily resolved: Is there any possible reconciliation between fidelity and freedom? And if so, at what price?"[68] Fidelity and freedom aside, this was a relationship noted for its "price":

there is one question [Sartre and I] have deliberately avoided: How would the third person feel about our arrangement? It often happened that the third person accommodated himself to it without difficulty. . . . But if the protagonist wanted more, then conflicts would break out. . . . This defect in our system manifested itself with particular acuity during the period I am now relating.[69]

Algren paid a great price, struggling with her for about ten years, in one way or the other, until they seemed to come to a sort of resolution (but only out of old age, according to Beauvoir).[70] Yet, when she published *Force of Circumstance*, the work which contained much of this story, and identified Algren, he bitterly denounced her for telling it.

The other affair, with Claude Lanzmann, was an extremely happy one; she and Lanzmann lived together for about five years (1952–57), something she had never done with Sartre. Beauvoir tells us something (though not as much as one would expect) of the quality of that relationship, but little about its beginning or ending. It was remarkable for its gaiety, and because it helped her through fears of aging and death. "Thanks to him," she said, "a thousand things were restored to me: joys, astonishments, anxieties, laughter and the freshness of the world."[71] But just as mysteriously as it had begun—"my telephone rang; 'I'd like to take you to the movies,' Lanzmann said")[72]—it ended. "Lanzmann and I drifted apart. It was natural, it was inevitable and even, on reflection, desirable for both of us; but the moment for reflection had not yet come. . . . the business of separation was difficult for me; for him, too, though the initiative had been his,"[73] she tells us. Without further comment, she closes her discussion of the only romantic relationship in which she lived with a man. Theagenus/Simone, "both mind and memory, the essential Subject," chose to bring minimal authorship or memory to this particular subject.[74]

The companionate self, a passion for Beauvoir dating back from her childhood love of Zaza, nearly resulted in the disappearance of her self. In a relationship without romantic love, she could maintain her role as the One and Only, for example, as the elder "master" to her younger sister. But with her passionate love for Zaza and then Sartre, the One and Only was transformed into its negative, a relative being. In the early relationship she created with Sartre, however, as she attempted to achieve a type of subjectivity through the "we," her self once again dramatically disappeared in the other. Eventually then, Beauvoir and Sartre became primarily intellectual companions; the roles of critic and editor for each other overshadowed their earlier passion. Thus, though she reported Zaza's death and Jacques' death, and performed the "on-paper" killing of Olga, she never had to kill Sartre. But she did create a work in which she reported how, over a ten-year period, he killed himself. The work, *Adieux: A Farewell to Sartre*, published after his death, opens with her statement: "This is the first of my books—the only one no doubt—that you will not have read before it is printed. It is wholly and entirely devoted to you; and you are not affected by it."[75] Theagenus/Simone, "both mind and memory, the essential Subject," lived on to narrate another tragic story.[76]

NOTES

1. Simone de Beauvoir, *Memoirs of a Dutiful Daughter*, trans. James Kirkup (New York: Harper Colophon Books, 1974), p. 91. (Hereafter, *Memoirs*.)

2. *Memoirs*, p. 91.

3. *Memoirs*, p. 94.

4. *Memoirs*, pp. 112–3. A misleading translation for *"Je me classais d'ordinaire avant elle"* in Simone de Beauvoir, *Mémoires d'une jeune fille rangée* (Paris: Gallimard, 1958), p. 114.

5. *Memoirs*, p. 95. Kirkup's choice of "waterfalling cataract" for *"l'eau des cascades"* is redundant and a bit stilted; better would be "cascading water," or "waterfall."

6. *Memoirs*, pp. 95–6. In Simone de Beauvoir, *The Prime of Life*, trans. Peter Green (Cleveland: World Publishing Company/Meridian Books, 1966), p. 24, as she describes the early years of her relationship with Sartre, she notes a similar concern for the effect of his death on her: "I knew that no harm could ever come to me from him—unless he were to die before I died."

7. *Memoirs*, p. 118.

8. *Memoirs*, p. 113.

9. *Memoirs*, p. 114. *"J'aimais mieux posséder l'univers qu'une figure"* could have been translated: "I preferred to possess the whole universe rather than have one specific character." *Mémoires*, p. 115.

10. *Memoirs*, p. 240.

11. *Memoirs*, p. 258.

12. *Memoirs*, pp. 276–7.

13. *Memoirs*, p. 280.

14. *Memoirs*, pp. 277–8.

15. *Memoirs*, p. 278.

16. *Memoirs*, p. 282.

17. *Memoirs*, p. 360.

18. The discussion is true to the academic format of the autobiography in Simone de Beauvoir's *All Said and Done*, trans. Patrick O'Brian (New York: G. P. Putnam's, 1974), p. 3. (Hereafter, *ASD*.) "I do not intend to lead the reader through a waking dream that might bring my past back to life, but to examine my history from the standpoint of certain given concepts and notions," she says.

19. *ASD*, p. 8.

20. *ASD*, p. 9.

21. *ASD*, p. 7.

22. On André, see *Memoirs*, p. 249. The full story of Zaza's trauma before her death remained unclear to Beauvoir (but most others directly involved at the time knew) until after she published *Memoirs*; then, one of Zaza's sisters visited her to explain the whole story. Unbeknownst to Maurice Merleau-Ponty himself, he was born as the result of an adulterous relationship. He learned this only through Zaza's family, who discovered it during routine investigations for Zaza's and his betrothal. This made their marriage impossible, in her family's eyes. See Claude Francis and Fernande Gontier, *Simone de Beauvoir: A Life . . . A Love Story*, trans. Lisa Nesselson (New York: St. Martin's Press, 1987), pp. 86–8.

23. *Memoirs*, p. 326. Feminist theory in recent years (since the early 1980s at least) has critiqued the notion of independence and increasingly substituted discussions of "interdependence" (Chodorow, Gilligan, Ruddick, etc.). Beauvoir was writing before these developments in feminist theory, and from her own perspectives—existentialism, and the feminism she developed in *The Second Sex*.

24. *Memoirs*, p. 233.

25. *Memoirs*, p. 348.

26. *Memoirs*, p. 348.

27. *Memoirs*, p. 345.

28. *Memoirs*, p. 344.

29. Simone de Beauvoir, *Force of Circumstance*, trans. Richard Howard (New York: Harper Colophon Books, 1977), p. 644. (Hereafter, *Force*.)

30. *Force*, p. 644.

31. *Force*, p. 644.

32. *Memoirs*, p. 345.

33. *Memoirs*, p. 92.

34. *Memoirs*, p. 345.

35. *Prime*, p. 54.

36. *Prime*, p. 54.

37. Simone de Beauvoir, *The Ethics of Ambiguity*, trans. Bernard Frechtman (New York: Citadel Press, 1970), p. 65. (Hereafter, Ethics.) Here Beauvoir's analysis is close to Jean-Paul Sartre's analysis of love in *Being and Nothingness: A Phenomenological Essay on Ontology*, trans. Hazel E. Barnes (New York: Washington Square Press, 1966). In this and other passages, the use of the male generic ("he," to refer to human beings in general) is jarring. Sometimes it occurs in the translation, but other times it is in Beauvoir's original.

38. *Ethics*, p. 64.

39. *Ethics*, p. 65.

40. *Prime*, p. 24.

41. *Prime*, p. 269.

42. *Prime*, p. 269.

43. Simone de Beauvoir, *The Second Sex*, trans. H. M. Parshley (New York: Vintage, 1989), p. 720.

44. *Prime*, pp. 269–70.

45. *Prime*, p. 193–4.

46. *Prime*, pp. 270–1.

47. *Prime*, p. 269.

48. *Prime*, p. 206.

49. Carol Ascher, *Simone de Beauvoir: A Life of Freedom* (Boston: Beacon Press, 1981), pp. 35 and 38–58, et passim.

50. Madeleine Gobeil, "Sartre Talks of Beauvoir," an interview with Jean-Paul Sartre, trans. Bernard Frechtman, *Vogue*, July 1965, pp. 72–3.

51. *Prime*, pp. 21–2 and 26-7, et passim.

52. *Prime*, p. 26.

53. *Prime*, p. 118.

54. *Prime*, p. 23.

55. *Prime*, p. 208.

56. *Prime*, p. 209.

57. *Prime*, p. 54.

58. Simone de Beauvoir, *La Force de l'âge* (Paris: Gallimard, 1960), p. 66. Italics and trans. mine. *"Castor"* (Beaver) was Sartre's French nickname for Beauvoir, though it originated with someone else, a friend named "André Herbaud" (possibly a pseudonym), one of Sartre's clique of three at the École Normale. Beauvoir relates its history: "At the beginning, he used to call me, affectionately, 'Mademoiselle.' One day he wrote on my exercise-book, in large capital letters: BEAUVOIR=BEAVER. 'You are a beaver,' he said. 'Beavers like company and they have a constructive bent.'" *Memoirs*, p. 323.

59. *Prime*, p. 54.

60. *Prime*, p. 9.

61. *Prime*, p. 15.

62. *Prime*, p. 178.

63. *Prime*, p. 452.

64. Alice Schwarzer, *After "The Second Sex": Conversations with Simone de Beauvoir*, trans. Marianne Howarth (New York: Pantheon Books, 1984), pp. 37 and 59.

65. *Prime*, p. 452.

66. *Prime*, p. 291.

67. See epilogue, *Force*, pp. 643–58.

68. *Force*, p. 124.

69. *Force*, p. 125.

70. *Force*, p. 509.

71. *Force*, p. 285.

72. *Force*, p. 279.

73. *Force*, p. 454.

74. *Memoirs*, p. 114.

75. Simone de Beauvoir, *Adieux: A Farewell to Sartre*, trans. Patrick O'Brian (New York: Pantheon Books, 1984), p. 3.

76. *Memoirs*, p. 114.

6

Writing the Self: The Writer

Although she decided that teaching would be her job, a choice that was a practical response to her need to support herself, Beauvoir is careful to tell us that writing was her "calling." In this, she and Sartre were well-matched; "We belonged to no place or country, no class, profession, or generation. Our truth lay elsewhere . . . inscribed upon the face of eternity, and the future would reveal it: we were writers," she says.[1] In the early days, she and Sartre saw writing as the embodiment of what they called their "radical freedom": "we imagined ourselves to be wholly independent agents. . . . To be a writer, to create—this was an adventure scarcely to be embarked upon without a conviction of absolute self-mastery, absolute control over ends and means."[2] Beauvoir's tone indicates that she is judging these past selves according to the philosophical notions developed in *Being and Nothingness* and *The Ethics of Ambiguity*, and that they were mistakenly defining themselves as pure freedom, without the facticity which also defines human existence.

In *Memoirs,* there are numerous introspective passages about her desire to become a writer, and specifically a writer who uses autobiographical material; these passages serve as examples of introspection. Beauvoir informs the reader that the combination of narrator and self-narrator appealed to her from early childhood, saying, "I knew how to use language, and as it expressed the essence of things, it illuminated them for me. I had a spontaneous urge to turn everything that happened to me into a story."[3] It was also her intention to achieve a kind of immortality by writing: "If I was describing in words an episode in my life, I felt that it was being rescued from oblivion, that it would interest others, and so be saved from extinction."[4] Though she claims here that it is the *event* and not the *self* which will be saved, later in a passage from *The Prime of Life*, recalling Camus' positive reaction to her novel, *The Blood of Others*, upon his reading a typescript of it, the *self* becomes the issue:

he drew me aside and said enthusiastically, "It's a *fraternal* book," and I thought: If a fraternity can be created by words, then writing is well worthwhile. What I wanted was to penetrate so deeply into other people's lives that when they heard my voice they would get the impression they were talking to themselves. If my words multiplied through millions of human hearts, it seemed to me that my existence, though reshaped and transfigured, would still, in a manner of speaking, survive.[5]

This is a peculiar passage; Camus' remark undoubtedly was meant to carry a *political* meaning, to claim that *The Blood of Others* was indeed a "Resistance novel," high praise from one who was a participant in that Resistance. Camus' word, "fraternal," an unusual adjective for a literary work, indicates that he felt it had the ability to create a sense of solidarity of "the people" against those oppressing them—in this particular case, the fascists.[6] But though she appreciated the comment, she seemed to miss the point, turning it to her own purpose; if the author wrote a "fraternal book," she would "survive," would be saved from extinction.[7]

LIFE REBOUNDS INTO LITERATURE

Beauvoir had written two long novels which she never tried to publish, and then a book of five stories about women, *La Primauté du spirituel*, for which she was unable to find a publisher. (The book has been published in recent years.)[8] As the years passed, she was producing no publishable writing—unlike Sartre:

I wanted to be a writer. . . . I had sworn to complete my great, all-revealing work at the age of twenty-two; yet when I embarked upon the first of my published novels, *She Came to Stay*, I was already thirty. In the family . . . the whisper went around that I was a *fruit sec*; my father remarked irritably that if I had something inside me, why couldn't I hurry up and get it out?[9]

Later, she judged that when she finally wrote and published a successful book at the age of thirty, *She Came to Stay*, her ability to produce it had to do with events in her life, not with anything that might be called "writing ability"; as she says, "I do not believe that my lack of [writing] experience can suffice to explain so prolonged a failure: I was hardly more professional when I began writing *She Came to Stay*. Must I, then, admit that whereas previously I had nothing to say, I had now 'found a subject'?"[10] The conclusion she came to about her own writing led her to a theory about literature, specifically about the necessary and sometimes painful connection between literature and life, rather than to the simplistic explanation that she had finally "found a subject":

Literature is born when something in life goes slightly adrift. In order to write . . . the first essential condition is that *reality should no longer be taken for granted*; only then can one both perceive it, and make others do so. . . . when [my] happiness was threatened . . . I rediscovered a certain kind of solitude in anxiety. The unfortunate episode of the trio did much more than supply me with a subject for a novel; it enabled me to deal with it (*elle me donna la possibilité de le traiter*).[11] [italics added]

In other words, the experience of the trio, as frightening as it had been for her, and ending with the need to "kill" Olga on paper, was the symptom of a problem and not the problem itself. That problem was the need to rediscover "a certain kind of solitude" by a diminishment of the "companionate self." With the anxiety brought about by the threat the trio represented to this type of self, she rediscovered "a certain kind of solitude" and a different kind of self. With this, she discovered the ability to write. The immediate problems of her life became the *solution* to the longstanding *problem* of the writer's failure to write. In a long footnote to this point, Beauvoir referred to this as "*cette notion de recul*," saying that everything she wrote thereafter confirmed it. This was the idea that certain life experiences "recoil" ("rebound" or "backfire") into literary works.[12]

In discussing the process of writing *The Blood of Others* (the book immediately following the "trio" novel), she made clear what her intentions in writing the book were:

I had finished *She Came to Stay* during the summer of 1941 . . . I was anxious to move on and discuss *the problems which were now foremost in my mind. The chief of these was still my relationship to the Other*; but I understood its complexity better than I had previously. My new hero, Jean Blomart, did not insist, as Françoise had done, on remaining the one sentient personality when confronted with other people. He refused to be a mere *object* where they were concerned, intervening in their lives with the brutal opacity of some inanimate thing; his problem was to . . . establish a clear relationship with them, involving freedom on both sides.[13] [italics added]

Beauvoir would use it to explore the problem that most concerned her, self and other. The difference between *She Came to Stay* and *The Blood of Others* was that at the writing of the second novel, because the "companionate self" she had formed with Sartre was not as powerful a force, she could have a *self*, and one with a specific "problem." Writing then became a mode of working on the problem, since the emotional break that was the result of the trio made it possible to discourse on it (*"de le traiter"*). When she had started college at the age of seventeen, she thought it would be the beginning of a liberation, "a new life . . . and all barriers, all prison walls, were being broken down."[14] But this vision of liberation was accompanied by her familiar desire to combine life and story, she said. Earlier she had wanted to create stories from her life's events. Now she wanted to make her life into a story; "My life would be a beautiful story come true, a story I would make up as I went along," she wrote (using the verb *"se raconter,"* "to narrate oneself").[15]

THE PHENOMENOLOGICAL-EXISTENTIALIST WRITING OF A LIFE

At the end of a major introspective passage in *La Force de l'âge (The Prime of Life)*, she calls upon *"se raconter"* again, when she says, "One can never know oneself but only tell about (or narrate) oneself."[16] The fifty-two-year-old narrator, being both narrator and protagonist, insists that the only way to an understanding of the self is through the story of the life of the self, a "personal account" of the autobiographer/writer. Expanding on her earlier *"notion de recul,"* the idea that remarkable life experiences make literature possible, she notes that the self becomes accessible through the phenomenological description of the self, the elaboration of the many profiles of the self afforded by autobiography. The narrator of *Memoirs* had told us that the seventeen-year-old Simone had hoped to design a life that was a beautiful story, but that romantic seventeen-year-old's dream of the creation of a beautiful life is now subsumed under the fifty-two-year-old's understanding of the philosophi-cal complexity of understanding *what the self is*, as an object for conscious-ness.[17]

She also observes that, though she is a writer writing the story of her life, she prefers writing by "the fact," rather than by an "explanation," or someone's analysis of the facts. Mistrusting her own as well as others' analyses of facts, she prefers the reader alone to make her or his own analysis of them. This develops into a defense of the process of her autobiographical writing and its foundation in existential theory, with its emphasis on choice: "Doubtless a prior condition of my taking an interest in Olga was the fact that I was free to do so."[18] She uses the freedom of the writer to present a self by its profiles, following the theory of the transcendental ego presented by Husserl and Sartre, according to which "the self is only a probable object, and that which says 'I' is known only by profiles."[19] However, this exposé is not an explanation; rather it follows from her claim that one can never *know* oneself, but only can *tell* (of) oneself.

In the introduction to *Force of Circumstance*, she completes the phenomenological move. Her life is an object; her self-life-writing is not "a work of art," but merely the description of an object (thus it is a phenomenological pursuit), albeit one with freedom (thus it is a pursuit that can be labeled "existentialist"):

> I make no claim to [this book's] being—any more than its predecessor—*a work of art*. . . . No; not a work of art, but my life with its enthusiasms and disappoint-ments. . . I believe in our freedom, our responsibility, but whatever their importance, this dimension of our existence eludes description. What can be described is merely our conditioning; I seem to my own eyes an object . . . I prefer to fathom rather than to flatter myself.[20]

This is one of a series of remarkable *introspective* passages that appear in Beauvoir's autobiographies; one commentator has called them "*bilans*," or balance sheets, by which she summarizes, takes stock of, and often defends her autobiographical project, hoping to clarify it for the reader.[21] The reader meets a doubly reflected Beauvoirian self in these, since the main or *retrospective* narrative is the "original" reflection on the self. These passages provide the richest discussions of her writing, as well as lucid commentary on her life in general.

The preface to *The Prime of Life* has a dual purpose: to introduce the second volume of autobiography and to explain the first, for the question that arose at the end of *Memoirs* was: for what had she used the freedom won in her battle against her bourgeois background and environment? It was simply this: to write. She is a writer and, by telling her own story, she can explain how writers write and why they write what they choose to write. So her second volume was written to show how one particular case and writing career, hers, came to be. From it, others can learn more and better about the career of writing than from a discussion in "abstract and general" terms.[22] As an existential-phenomenologist, she finds value in narrating the progress and development of her writing career concretely and in a specific way; "Why those books and not some others? . . . useless to have told the story of my vocation as a writer if I don't try to tell how it was realized."[23] In the general terms of both existentialism and phenomenology, this is a respectable undertaking. The choice to explain her life as a writer by its details rather than in generalities is a phenomenological project, for she is presenting a phenomenon, her life, a particular writer's life, through its "profiles," which Husserl had insisted on for the phenomenological description of any object.

Beauvoir's preface reveals the existential self in a number of ways. As we have seen, the freedom of the for-itself is its "content," and this content is not a substance; it is the nothingness of freedom as intentionality, a negativity, but certainly not a passivity. Beauvoir ties together the end of *Memoirs* with the beginning of *The Prime of Life* by using this concept of freedom. She "won" freedom at the end of her adolescence, also the endpoint of *Memoirs*: by eluding the "revolting fate" ("*destin fangeux*") which awaited her, she had realized her freedom.[24] Remembered again at the beginning of *The Prime of Life*, this is the freedom of the existential self, the for-itself: "Freedom I had—but freedom to do what? What new direction would the course of my life take as a result of all this fuss and commotion, the pitched battle that had culminated in victorious release?"[25] Because of how tightly she linked these two pieces (the ending of *Memoirs* and the preface to *The Prime of Life*), we can easily see Beauvoirian ethics unfolding, in her own story of her life. There are three important points, and they echo those made in *Ethics*: (1) freedom must be won; it is not a given, (2) it is in the adolescent stage that the for-itself understands that this freedom must be won, and (3) freedom is always concretely realized (in her case, first by her disconnection from the bourgeoisie, then by her writing). The point of existential ethics at stake here is that the self *is* free, but that the self must take responsibility for *becoming* free. For Beauvoir, the important point is the "responsibility for," or the "assumption of" freedom, which she explained in *Ethics*. This point is stressed throughout *The Second Sex*, a book which both details the oppression of women by patriarchal society, and nevertheless maintains that women must take responsibility, in order to "assume" their freedom (whether that be through, for example, supporting rape crisis centers, refusing traditional marriages, or fighting for reproductive freedom of all kinds). They must free themselves from the "revolting fate" which awaits them.

In writing *The Second Sex*, Beauvoir's philosophy was transformed into her own brand of "existentialism," feminist existentialism (or existential feminism), which includes a Hegelian stress on the self-other dialectic as well as including a gendered notion of the for-itself; whether this still results in "existentialist philosophy" would certainly depend on the definition of existentialist philosophy one used. But there were direct historical connections between this new philosophy she forged and her own autobiographical project, because *The Second Sex* was begun in preparation for her writing of her autobiography; it is virtually a preface to her autobiography, as I already noted earlier in this book:

I wanted to write about myself . . . the first question to come up was: What has it meant to me to be a woman? . . . *it was a revelation*: this world was a masculine world, my childhood had been nourished by myths forged by men, and I hadn't reacted to them in at all the same way I should have done if I had been a boy. I was so interested in this discovery that I abandoned my project for a personal confession in order to give all my attention to finding out about the condition of woman in its broadest terms.[26] [italics added]

Richard Howard's translation misses something here; Beauvoir's remark was: "*Je regardai et j'eus une revelation*," that is, "I looked and I had a revelation."[27] This sharpens for the reader the experience of the thinker/writer, Beauvoir, from whose self-writing this passage is taken; "I had a revelation" more clearly points to an active self than "it was a revelation."

AUTOBIOGRAPHICAL PROMISES AND TRUTHS

In *All Said and Done*, Beauvoir discusses the reaction to the lines with which *Force of Circumstance* ends (and surely, by now, the most quoted lines in her entire autobiographical work): "The promises have all been kept. And yet turning an incredulous gaze toward that young and credulous girl, I realize with stupor how much I was gypped."[28] In *All Said and Done*, Beauvoir explains this passage by an explanation of what writing is, particularly autobiography. She had agreed with Francis Jeanson when he suggested that, in that much quoted line, she had "yielded to a kind of 'literary dramatization,'" and she notes that readers don't always understand or take account of the difference between the writer as a person and the fictitious literary "character" created even in autobiography, a character which "transcends time," and for whom "the present is tantamount to eternity."[29]

In this and other passages, Beauvoir provides detailed descriptions of how she came to write the books she did, the ambivalences, vacillation, and losses of nerve that she experienced before and during the production of the books, as well as her reactions to the responses to her books, and her ideas of what the practice of writing is. She fulfills the promise she made in the preface to *The Prime of Life*, when she determined that the major reason to continue her autobiography after *Memoirs* was to show the public the details of a writer's life, and not just to discuss the generalities.

In the last several pages of Part One of *The Prime of Life*, Beauvoir gives the reader a new perspective on her life. She has written of events up to the spring of 1939 and finds a natural stopping place for the narrative. She is about to relate a stage of her life which was enormously significant for her, since it was the beginning of her political/historical awareness. Similarly, in *Memoirs*, the year 1929 marked several important events in her life: the end of her formal education, her economic emancipation, her leaving her "paternal home," the ending of old friendships, and the meeting with Sartre. The year 1939 would also mark an important moment, the movement from youth to maturity.[30]

Beauvoir had envisioned a particular form of writing (novel writing) as her life's project, and for a particular reason:

in my opinion this medium [novels] surpassed all others . . . like George Eliot, who had become identified in my mind with Maggie Tulliver, I would myself become an imaginary character, endowed with beauty, desirability, and a sort of shimmering transparent loveliness. It was this metamorphosis that my ambition sought. I was alive, and still am, to reflections everywhere, in windows, rippling over water, and would watch them for minutes on end, in a state of charmed fascination. I dreamed of splitting into two selves (*me dédoubler*), and of having a shadowy alter ego that would pierce and haunt people's hearts.[31]

So she hoped to create another self through novel writing, a phantom self.[32] Yet an earlier phantom, Zaza, had been lurking, haunting her ("*souvent la nuit elle m'est apparue, toute jaune*")[33] until she finally was released from Zaza, by writing her own autobiography. Relating the story of the reception of *Memoirs*, her first autobiography, Beauvoir notes:

I was spurred on by the success of my *Memoirs* which . . . affected me more intimately than the reception of any of my other books. . . . Ghosts rose up out of the past, some annoyed, some kindly. . . . The Mabille family were grateful to me for having made Zaza live again. . . . It was romantic, this discovery of my past brought about by my writing an account of it. As I reread Zaza's letters and notebooks, I was plunged back into it once more. And it was as though she had died a second time. Never again did she come back to see me in my dreams.[34]

Beauvoir discovered her own past by writing her autobiography; she was haunted by ghosts because of it; she resuscitated at least one dead person, Zaza, by writing it; but that person finally "died" because of it.[35]

Earlier, Beauvoir had wanted writing to save her from extinction. The immortality that writing and being read can produce was mentioned again, in *The Prime of Life*, as she discussed her decision to write *Memoirs*:

I had long wanted to set down the story of my first twenty years; nor did I ever forget the distress signals which my adolescent self sent out to the older woman who was afterward to absorb me. . . . Nothing, I feared, would survive of that girl, not so much as a pinch of ashes. I begged her successor to recall my youthful ghost, one day, from the limbo to which it had been consigned. Perhaps the only reason for writing my books was to make this . . . possible. When I was fifty . . . the time had come. I took *that child* and *that adolescent girl*, both so long given up for lost in the depths of the unrecalled past, and endowed them with my adult awareness. I gave them *a new existence*—in black and white, on sheets of paper.[36] [italics added]

These last sentences are philosophically and literarily richer in Beauvoir's French than Green's English translation indicates. Beauvoir wrote: *"j'ai prêté ma conscience à l'enfant, à la jeune fille abandonnée au fond du temps perdu, et perdues avec lui. Je les ai fait exister en noir et blanc sur du papier."*[37] The translation should have included a philosophical term for *conscience* and should have revealed the literary allusion to Proust in *"du temps perdu,"* so that the reader could make the relevant connections. It would read better like this: "I took that child . . . and . . . adolescent girl . . . lost in the depths of unremembered times past, and directed my consciousness to them. I made them exist in black and white on paper."[38] Beauvoir's use in this last sentence of the verb *"exister"* indicates that she consciously understood that writing, and autobiographical writing in particular, was not the story of her "self" (i.e., the present for-itself consciously engaged in the task of writing), but rather the creation of characters, as in a novel—child, young woman—a creation made possible by Beauvoir's "lending" them her present consciousness, the freedom that is activated through and in the process of writing. This passage provides additional evidence to disprove Lejeune's claim (discussed earlier) that Beauvoir simplistically believed in the "past-in-itself."

Regarding the referential component of autobiography, Julia Kristeva makes some brief but rather harsh remarks about Beauvoir's autobiographical writing, elaborately complimenting her for her "naive cruelty" and "austere and cutting pen."[39] Kristeva excludes herself from the class of those skilled at autobiography, claiming that her own psychoanalytic experience makes it impossible for her to be a "good witness," since *she* understands the gap between "what is said" and "undecidable 'truth.'"[40] (In spite of this, she writes an autobiographical essay.) She implies that Beauvoir assumed her memoirs were directly referential to the "truth." This critique speaks to the retrospective dimension of Beauvoir's autobiographies but overlooks many introspective passages in them, passages in which Beauvoir discusses and problematizes the act of writing in general, and the practice of autobiography in particular. One would expect a more sensitive reading from Kristeva than this.

WRITING FOR AND AGAINST THE SELF

In *Force of Circumstance*, Beauvoir once again explains why she decided to continue her autobiography. Such explanations become more valuable for her readers if they aren't read primarily as defenses of her autobiographical project, but as opportunities she created to write about writing. In *Force*, there is an important change of viewpoint on the purpose of autobiography, as she defended her haste: "the indifference of decrepitude would keep me from grasping my subject . . . I wanted my blood to circulate in this narrative; I wanted to fling myself into it, still very much alive—to put myself in question before all questions are silenced."[41] Here, Beauvoir presents another function of autobiography. Autobiography is an action by and for the present self, the for-itself. In asserting this, she is acknowledging the continual creation of the self through the autobiography, because the autobiography is an activity of the self, taken in the existential sense of a "self" as a for-itself, an openness, a nothingness capable of action. Autobiography is discourse as well as description; as such, it has the potential to be a presence of the self to itself, rather than merely the presentation of an object, a past self, because of the nature of the for-itself, because of its openness, its ability "to put [one]self into question before all questions are silenced."

By contrast, in the prologue to the final autobiographical volume, *All Said and Done*, published in 1972, when Beauvoir was sixty-four years old, she talks of making an accounting of a life through autobiography, rather than allowing autobiography to continue the life. The reader senses that this autobiography will raise no questions for the author; she thinks there is only one important question left: how and when she will die. Indeed, she sounds finished. She tells us that without a goal, she is "slipping inevitably towards [the] grave."[42] Unlike the title of the third volume, *La Force des choses* ("the force of circumstance"), which called attention to the for-itself in the world, enmeshed in "circumstance," in the various matters, details, business, and contingencies that a life aware of what she called "History" offers, the very title of the last volume indicates closure: "all said and done," that is, *"tout compte fait,"* "all accounts settled." In contradiction to the notion of the self as for-itself, a nonsubstance, a never-finished openness, Beauvoir asserts here that her life, hence her self, is not an openness any longer, and she awaits the inevitable and ultimate closure, death, a factual closure to accompany the existential closure she is not only voicing but creating by articulating it through the practice of autobiography. She has forgotten the existentialism of *The Ethics of Ambiguity* and her own assertion that the for-itself is not a thing.

Beauvoir's explanation of her autobiographical project in *All Said and Done* departed from existentialist themes remarkably, but already in *The Prime of Life*, she was consciously departing from them: "this project interested me in itself. My existence is not finished, but already it possesses a sense which in all likelihood the future will scarcely modify. . . . Now is the time, or never, to *learn* it" [italics added].[43] Here she both admits and denies that the for-itself is its future, thus she denies the nothingness of the for-itself as she had described it. She begins to treat her self as if she were a fact to be *learned* rather than an existence to be actively lived and defined in the living. It is interesting that the second part of *Force of Circumstance* begins with the story of her love affair with Claude Lanzmann, an event that seems to have surprised her:

Young women have an acute sense of what . . . should not be done when one is no longer young. . . . When I was thirty I made the same sort of resolution: "Certain aspects of love, well, after forty, one has to give them up." . . . [I] promised myself that when I reached that stage, I would dutifully retire to the shelf. . . . Now, at forty-four, I was relegated to the land of shades; yet . . . when the opportunity arose of coming back to life, I seized it gladly.[44]

Here, Beauvoir slips into the ideology she attacked in *The Second Sex*: that woman is a sexual object patriarchally defined as Other, rather than a subject/self to be treated as such, and this is worse for the "older" and supposedly nonsexual woman. Twenty years later, she seemed convinced that she was more positivity than negativity, the closer she moved to death. In *All Said and Done* she narrated not her existence but her essence, writing thematically rather than in her usual fashion (a generally chronological treatment interspersed with introspection); she presents her life in this volume as a "work," a book to be dissected according to themes. Being a good scholar, she will dutifully carry out the intellectual exercise of finding the themes and documenting them through the "relevant passages" of her life. Moving away from her existence to her essence, Beauvoir may have hoped that this autobiography would help her to die.

ETHICAL WRITING

In *The Prime of Life*, Beauvoir emphasizes the importance of the change that took place in her life starting in 1939, as "History" entered her life; this was what she called her "moral period."[45] She remarks that, as questionable as it is to divide one's life up into sections, she will do that because of the tremendous change she went through at this point in her life, as it was transformed by the presence of History. As *she* uses the term, History refers to a complexity of relationships, not a linear succession of events or a series of causes and effects. It is the flow of certain events as those events are explained through power and class relations within nations, as well as colonial struggles and resistance movements against instituted powers (later, this would include feminism, the movement against patriarchal power). This was the period in her life when she achieved political and social awareness and saw beyond the borders of her own happiness, toward an understanding of the problems and solutions affecting the happiness of others, particularly oppressed others. She also came to understand both that she herself was a historical being and that her life, any life, is part of a world, a community of individuals, and a flow of activity which is not entirely in one's own control.[46] In terms of the existentialist notion of the self developed in *Ethics*, Beauvoir was claiming that with this part of her life she began an ethical life: "There we have an irreducible truth. The me-others relationship is as indissoluble as the subject-object relationship. . . . To will oneself free is also to will others free."[47]

She credits this change not to political involvement, but to the very *individual* act of writing, that is, to the process of the writing of her first novel, *L'Invitée* (*She Came to Stay*). The years during which she wrote it, 1938 to 1941, also marked the beginning of World War II in Europe. In writing this novel, a *roman à clef*, she began to distinguish that past self she described in the character of Françoise from her then present self. The past self of Simone was concerned with her own personal happiness and individual relationships exclusively, but then she changed: "Then, suddenly, History burst over me, and I dissolved into fragments. I woke to find myself scattered over the four quarters of the globe, linked by every nerve in me to each and every other individual," she states.[48] She reiterates the critical nature of this point later in the book, when she refers to it as the beginning of her "moral period."[49]

Throughout the continuation of World War II, Beauvoir's own self became further historicized, socialized, and aware of its own mortality.[50] With this change, perhaps because of it, came the acknowledgment of the human condition: its ambiguity and its mortality, both of which are themes we find in *Ethics*.[51] This awareness was both created and acted upon by the activity of writing:

Misfortune and misery had erupted into the world, and literature had become as essential to me as the very air I breathed. . . . What I *had* experienced . . . was the pathetic ambiguity of our human condition . . . I felt the need to write, in order to do justice to a truth with which all my emotional impulses were out of step.

. . . each book thenceforth impelled me toward its successor, for the more I saw of the world, the more I realized that it was brimming over with all I could ever hope to experience, understand, and put into words.[52]

By the end of the war, the change in her was complete. In a sense, and without knowing it, she was becoming the ethical person she would write about in *Ethics* two years later. She describes herself at this period in the following manner: "Events had changed me; what Sartre used to call my 'divided mind' had finally yielded before the unanswerable arguments that reality had brought against it. I was at last prepared to admit that *my life was not a story of my own telling*, but a compromise between myself and the world at large."[53] [italics added] Here she purposely refers to the statement she made in *Memoirs* when, by contrast, she had said of her earlier life plans: "My life would be a beautiful story come true, a story I would make up as I went along."[54] But by the end of the war, her life was bound up with others, political action beckoned, she began to see her life connected to others' lives, and "freedom, oppression, the happiness and [human] misery" concerned her personally.[55]

"A LIFE . . . SUCH A STRANGE OBJECT"

In an important reflective passage in *The Prime of Life*, she makes the only direct explication in the autobiographies of her notion of the self. She affirms her belief ("still," she says) in the theory of the "transcendental ego."[56] As we saw earlier, she also claims that the self ("*le moi*") is grasped through "profiles." Because the English translation renders "*profils*" as "outer edge" here, it conceals the phenomenological analysis in the passage. Alluding to Husserl's notion that any object is delivered over through its profiles, in discussing the self Beauvoir says that it is an object with profiles—albeit a "probable object"—since the self is an object with an "inside." As an object and therefore as something seen through its profiles, the self is more easily and better seen by others, that is, from the outside. An actual cognizing of this special object, the self, by itself is really impossible. That is the reason she claims that "one can never know oneself but only tell about (narrate) oneself."[57] Unlike the Cartesian move by which consciousness, the thinking power, becomes the self, Beauvoir here uses the phenomenological analysis of the self, which is to say that it is a byproduct of consciousness, an object for it.

When Carol Ascher, a very good biographer of Beauvoir, comments on this passage, she displays not only a lack of patience with the philosophical underpinnings of Beauvoir's writing, but also a lack of sensitivity to their subtleties. Ascher wants the boundaries of "autobiography" and "philosophy" clearly drawn and kept separate. Her critique also displays a lack of attention to the French original. Using quotations from *The Prime of Life*, she says, "In fact, with her usual capacity to give her idiosyncrasies philosophical language, de Beauvoir insists that an individual only 'grasps the outer edge' of him or herself; 'an outsider can get a clearer and more accurate picture.'" [58] In a note, Ascher connects Beauvoir's ideas on the self to Sartre's position "that consciousness cannot pin itself down." She contends that, like most philosophical positions, this position developed out of the personal idiosyncracies of the philosopher (Sartre) to explain and justify his own notions and positions, and Ascher concludes that Beauvoir and Sartre shared idiosyncracies. Though such a conclusion may be true, it is debatable, and based on a premise impossible to prove satisfactorily ("a philosophical position develops out of the personal idiosyncracies of its creator"), and one that could be extended to include other groups, even biographers.

But Ascher's summary also ignores the phenomenological core of Beauvoir's passage: to narrate the self is to describe an object. As is true of any object, when the for-itself becomes an object through the reflection imposed by autobiography, it can only be grasped through its profiles ("outer edges" in the English translation). Beauvoir's claim is intended, I believe, as evidence of her attention to phenomenological tenets and not, as Ascher claims, to her "running from selfhood."[59]

At the end of the first part of her next volume, *Force of Circumstance*, Beauvoir provides us with a description of a life that is also an elaboration of her notion of the self and an explanation of autobiography itself. To a writer of autobiography from the existential-phenomenological tradition as Beauvoir was, the self presents itself not simply as a life to be narrated, but also as an object to be known (phenomenology) and a freedom to be appreciated (existentialism). But the self/life is no ordinary object. Its description is difficult, since it exists continually in relation to a changeable world, as it (the for-itself) tries to describe itself and that world:

A life is such a strange object, at one moment translucent, at another utterly opaque, an object I make with my own hands, an object imposed on me, an object for which the world provides the raw material and then steals it from me again, pulverized by events, scattered, broken, scored yet retaining its unity; how heavy it is and how inconsistent: this contradiction breeds many misunderstandings.[60]

The autobiographical writer's task is to show both the breaks in the unity and the unity, in whatever ways possible. Beauvoir called upon a variety of autobiographical practices and techniques to do this: from *Memoirs*, which contains neither introductions nor an epilogue; to *The Prime of Life*, with a preface and several long, reflective, "intrusive" passages at the end of each of the book's two parts; to *Force of Circumstance*, which contains an introduction and an interlude as well as an epilogue; to *All Said and Done*, with its academic and thematic structure. Theagenus/Simone, "mind and memory, the essential Subject," had found her most engrossing subject: the self.

NOTES

1. Simone de Beauvoir, *The Prime of Life*, trans. Peter Green (Cleveland: World Publishing Company/Meridian Books, 1966), p. 22. (Hereafter, *Prime*.)

2. *Prime*, pp. 18–9.

3. Simone de Beauvoir, *Memoirs of a Dutiful Daughter*, trans. James Kirkup (New York: Harper Colophon Books, 1974), pp. 69–70. (Hereafter, *Memoirs*.)

4. *Memoirs*, p. 70.

5. *Prime*, p. 445. Camus' positive reaction to this book contrasts sharply with his inordinately negative reaction later to Beauvoir's *The Second Sex*, trans. H. M. Parshley (New York: Vintage, 1989).

6. See *Prime*, p. 428ff., for her discussion of Simone de Beauvoir, *The Blood of Others*, trans. Roger Senhouse and Yvonne Moyse (New York: Pantheon Books, 1983).

7. That *The Blood of Others* had a nonpolitical meaning for its author is clear, as Beauvoir discusses the reception of the book. In her *Force of Circumstance*, trans. Richard Howard (New York: Harper Colophon Books, 1977), p. 36, she says that to read the novel that way (i.e., politically) was a mistake: "*Blood of Others* was published in September; its main theme, as I have said, was the paradox of this existence experienced by me as my freedom and by those who came in contact with me as an object. This intention was not apparent to the public; the book was labeled a 'Resistance novel.'" The book was published immediately after the war was over in 1945. Later, in her *All Said and Done*, trans. Patrick O'Brian (New York: G. P. Putnam's, 1974), she also stated that she hoped to survive in her writing; "I also wanted to realize myself in books that, like those I had loved, would be existing objects for others, but objects haunted by a presence—my presence," she says. *ASD*, p. 29.

8. Referred to in *Prime* as *La Primauté du spirituel*, this was published as *Quand Prime le Spirituel* (Paris: Gallimard, 1979), because, as the editor notes in the English edition, p. 7, the original title had already been used by Jacques Maritain. The English translation, titled *When Things of the Spirit Come First*, was translated by Patrick O'Brian (New York: Pantheon, 1982). For Beauvoir's discussion of this, see *Prime*, pp. 178–81 and 261.

9. *Prime*, pp. 289–90.

10. *Prime*, p. 290.

11. *Prime*, p. 290. Green translates "*traiter*" as "deal with"; it can also mean treat, discuss, or discourse about. Simone de Beauvoir, *La Force de l'âge* (Paris: Gallimard, 1960), p. 374.

12. *La Force de l'âge*, p. 374. Green translates it fuzzily as "this 'revised perspective idea'" and puts the note into the main text. *Prime*, p. 290.

13. *Prime*, p. 428.

14. *Memoirs*, p. 169.

15. *Memoirs*, p. 169; Simone de Beauvoir, *Mémoires d'une jeune fille rangée* (Paris: Gallimard, 1958), p. 168. The reflexive here functions both in a subjective and objective way: "*je me raconte*" can mean "I tell me (the-story-of-myself)" and "I tell my story to myself." In English, this becomes a direct and indirect object, the direct object being the same entity as the subject—that is, the self, "I" and "me."

16. *La Force de l'âge*, p. 377. Trans. mine. There are several badly translated passages in this book; I use my own translations several times.

17. A cryptic formulation of the difficulty of telling stories of the past, whether autobiographical or historical, is the remark made by Fortune Teller in Thornton Wilder's "The Skin of Our Teeth: A Play in Three Acts," in *Three Plays by Thornton Wilder* (New York: Bantam, 1958), p. 100: "I tell the future. Nothing easier. But who can tell your past?"

18. *Prime*, p. 292.

19. *La Force de l'âge*, p. 377. Trans. mine.

20. *Force*, pp. vi–vii.

21. Terry Keefe, *Simone de Beauvoir: A Study of Her Writings* (Totowa, NJ: Barnes and Noble Books, 1983), p. 36.

22. *Force*, p. 10.

23. *La Force de l'âge*, pp. 9–10. Trans. mine.

24. *Memoirs*, p. 360; *Mémoires*, p. 359.

25. *Prime*, p. 9.

26. *Force*, pp. 94–5.

27. Simone de Beauvoir, *La Force des choses* (Paris: Gallimard, 1963), p. 109.

28. *Force*, p. 658.

29. *ASD*, pp. 117–8.

30. The passage is placed at the end of the first part of *Prime*, which covers the years 1929 to 1944.

31. *Prime*, pp. 290–1. *La Force de l'âge*, p. 375.

32. *La Force de l'âge*, p. 375.

33. *Mémoires*, p. 359.

34. *Force*, p. 463.

35. In two other places at least, she speaks of wanting to resuscitate Zaza. See *Prime*, p. 179 (*La Force de l'âge*, p. 231). Also see p. 6, in the author's preface (written when the book was published, more than forty years after the book had been written), *When Things of the Spirit Come First*, trans. Patrick O'Brian (New York: Pantheon, 1982): "In my drafts of novels I had already made vain attempts at bringing Zaza back to life. . . . In this book I kept closer to reality. *Anne*, at the age of twenty, was tormented by the same anguish and the same doubts as Zaza. Perhaps the only way of convincing the reader was to give an exact account of both, as I did in *Memoirs of a Dutiful Daughter*." Certainly, this autobiographical account was the one that convinced the *author*.

36. *Prime*, p. 9.

37. *La force de l'âge*, p. 9. Evidently, Green mistook *prendre* (take) for the word Beauvoir actually used here, *prêter* (lend, impart, attribute, bestow).

38. *Prime*, p. 9.

39. Julia Kristeva, "My Memory's Hyperbole," in Domna C. Stanton, ed., *The Female Autograph* (Chicago: The University of Chicago Press, 1987), p. 219.

40. Kristeva in Stanton, p. 219.

41. *Force*, p. v.

42. *ASD*, prologue, unnumbered.

43. *La Force de l'âge*, p. 10. Trans. mine; Green's makes philosophical connections impossible to see. He substituted the word "life" for the French "*existence*," a usage that would be adequate if the writer were not an existentialist philosopher.

44. *Force*, p. 279.

45. *Prime*, p. 433.

46. *Prime*, p. 285.

47. Simone de Beauvoir, *The Ethics of Ambiguity*, trans. Bernard Frechtman (New York: Citadel Press, 1970), pp. 72–3.

48. *Prime*, p. 295.

49. *Prime*, p. 433.

50. *Prime*, p. 474.

51. *Prime*, p. 479.

52. *Prime*, p. 479.

53. *Prime*, p. 385.

54. *Memoirs*, p. 169. Francis and Gontier use this statement as the epigraph to their biography of her. When she wrote this in 1958, it is possible that she was employing ironic detachment; she certainly wanted to indicate to her readers the intense romanticism with which the young Simone viewed her writing.

55. *Force*, p. 4.

56. *Prime*, p. 292. Beauvoir should have written "transcendent ego" here, rather than "transcendental ego." As it stands, this remark doesn't acknowledge Sartre's famous claim in *The Transcendence of the Ego*—and his attack on Husserl's ideas. This probably is just a case of careless terminology in Beauvoir's writing. The French reads: "*je crois encore aujourd'hui à la théorie de l'ego transcendantal'; le moi n'est qu'un objet probable, et celui qui dit je n'en saisit que des profils; autrui peut en avoir une vision plus nette ou plus juste.*" *La Force de l'âge*, p. 377.

57. *La Force de l'âge*, p. 377. Trans. mine. The English translation misses the phenomenology again, and confuses the logic. Peter Green phrased it: "self-knowledge is impossible, and the best one can hope for is self-revelation."

58. Carol Ascher, *Simone de Beauvoir: A Life of Freedom* (Boston: Beacon Press, 1981), p. 38.

59. Ascher, p. 38.

60. *Force*, p. 276.

Conclusion

Beauvoir's analysis in *The Second Sex* problematized the original existential-phenomenological notion of the self she had used in her earlier writings, which was the notion of the for-itself, because in *The Second Sex* Beauvoir showed that the self was also gendered. Consequently, in her description of woman, existentialism gave way, to some extent, to a type of empiricism. But, though she performed a study of woman in her theoretical writing, she made a study of one particular woman through her autobiographical writing about herself. This she did by calling upon both the existential-phenomenological self and the gendered self.

Because autobiography is a form of reflection on the self, existential-phenomenology would assume that autobiography could only produce a past self, since in its analysis, autobiography makes the for-itself into an in-itself, and conscious being begins to resemble a thing.

But autobiography is also discourse; as such, it has political and social dimensions. Beauvoir's writing of a multivolumed autobiography was a way of taking control of the story she had lived and was living with Sartre, a story in which, before this, she had always appeared as a secondary character. It was also a way of forming, in her own words, the tragic death of another person she loved, her friend, Zaza. Through autobiographical writing, she understood herself as no longer a relative being; she became "mind and memory," and finally "the essential Subject" of her relationships.

Beauvoir's reflection on her own life bears the mark of a thinker who wanted to preserve the tension between freedom and determinism which she had created in *The Second Sex*. Her own analysis in that work taught her that, being a woman, she was oppressed by patriarchy. But she used the philosophies of existentialism and phenomenology, as well as the politics of feminism, to create for herself a *praxis* for living and writing her woman-life. Assuming and accepting her subjectivity through the act of autobiographical writing, she created (and recreated) her freedom, by describing the concrete forms it took. In doing this, she made her freedom real, and realized that she was free.

Bibliography

PRIMARY SOURCES

Adieux: A Farewell to Sartre. Trans. Patrick O'Brian. New York: Pantheon Books, 1984.

All Said and Done. Trans. Patrick O'Brian. New York: G. P. Putnam's, 1974.

The Blood of Others. Trans. Roger Senhouse and Yvonne Moyse. New York: Pantheon Books, 1983.

Le Deuxième sexe. Paris: Gallimard, 1949.

The Ethics of Ambiguity. Trans. Bernard Frechtman. New York: Citadel Press, 1970.

"L'Existentialisme et la sagesse des nations." In *L'Existentialisme et la sagesse des nations.* Paris: Nagel, 1963.

La Force de l'âge. Paris: Gallimard, 1960.

La Force des choses. Paris: Gallimard, 1963.

Force of Circumstance: After the War. Vol. I. Trans. Richard Howard. New York: Harper Colophon Books, 1977.

Force of Circumstance: Hard Times. Vol. II. Trans. Richard Howard. New York: Harper Colophon Books, 1977.

Mémoires d'une jeune fille rangée. Paris: Gallimard, 1958.

Memoirs of a Dutiful Daughter. Trans. James Kirkup. New York: Harper Colophon Books, 1974.

"Merleau-Ponty et le pseudo-sartrisme." In *Privilèges.* Paris: Gallimard, 1955.

Pour une morale de l'ambiguité. Paris: Gallimard, 1974.

The Prime of Life. Trans. Peter Green. Cleveland: World Publishing Company/ Meridian Books, 1966.

Pyrrhus et Cinéas. Paris: Gallimard, 1944.

The Second Sex. Trans. H. M. Parshley. New York: Vintage, 1989.

She Came to Stay. Unattributed translation of *L'Invitée.* New York: World Publishing Company, 1954.

Tout compte fait. Paris: Gallimard, 1972.

When Things of the Spirit Come First: Five Early Tales. Trans. Patrick O'Brian. New York: Pantheon, 1982.

SECONDARY SOURCES

Ascher, Carol. *Simone de Beauvoir: A Life of Freedom.* Boston: Beacon Press, 1981.

Barnes, Hazel.   "Sartre's Concept of the Self."   *Review of Existential Psychology and Psychiatry* 17, no. 1 (1980–81): pp. 41–65.

Braun, Sidney D. *Dictionary of French Literature.* Greenwich, CT: Fawcett Premier Books, 1958.

Brueckner, John H., compiler and ed.   *Brueckner's French Contextuary.* Englewood Cliffs, NJ: Prentice-Hall, 1975.

Coe, Richard N. *When the Grass Was Taller: Autobiography and the Experience of Childhood.* New Haven, CT: Yale University Press, 1984.

Francis, Claude, and Fernande Gontier. *Simone de Beauvoir: A Life . . . a Love Story.* Trans. Lisa Nesselson. New York: St. Martin's Press, 1987.

Fullbrook, Kate, and Edward Fullbrook.   *Simone de Beauvoir and Jean-Paul Sartre: The Remaking of a Twentieth-Century Legend.* New York: HarperCollins, 1994.

Gobeil, Madeleine. "Sartre Talks of Beauvoir." Interview with Jean-Paul Sartre. Trans. Bernard Frechtman. *Vogue* (July 1965): pp. 72–3.

Hegel, G.W.F. *The Phenomenology of Mind.* Trans. J.B. Baillie. London: George Allen & Unwin LTD, 1964.

Heidegger, Martin. *Being and Time.* Trans. John Macquarrie and Edward Robinson. New York: Harper and Row, 1962.

Husserl, Edmund. *Ideas: General Introduction to Pure Phenomenology.* Trans. W. R. Boyce Gibson. New York: Collier Books, 1962.

Jay, Paul. *Being in the Text: Self-Representation from Wordsworth to Roland Barthes.* Ithaca, NY: Cornell University Press, 1984.

Keefe, Terry. *Simone de Beauvoir: A Study of Her Writings.* Totowa, NJ: Barnes and Noble Books, 1983.

Kristeva, Julia. "My Memory's Hyperbole." Trans. Athena Viscusi. In *The Female Autograph: Theory and Practice of Autobiography from the Tenth to the Twentieth Century,* ed. Domna C. Stanton. Chicago: University of Chicago Press, 1987, pp. 219–35.

LeDoeuff, Michèle. "Simone de Beauvoir and Existentialism." *Feminist Studies* 6 (1980): pp. 277–89.

Lejeune, Philippe. *Le Pacte autobiographique.* Paris: Seuil, 1975.

Marcel, Gabriel. "An Essay in Autobiography." In *The Philosophy of Existentialism.* Trans. Manya Harari. New York: Citadel Press, 1956, pp. 104–28.

Marcuse, Herbert. *One-Dimensional Man: Studies in the Ideology of Advanced Industrial Society*. Boston: Beacon Press, 1964.

Marks, Elaine. *Simone de Beauvoir: Encounters with Death*. New Brunswick, NJ: Rutgers University Press, 1973.

Morris, Phyllis Sutton. *Sartre's Concept of a Person: An Analytic Approach*. Amherst: University of Massachusetts Press, 1976.

Mueller, Janel. "Autobiography of a 'New Creatur': Female Spirituality, Selfhood, and Authorship in 'The Book of Margery Kempe.'" In *The Female Autograph: Theory and Practice of Autobiography from the Tenth to the Twentieth Century*, ed. Domna C. Stanton. Chicago: University of Chicago Press, 1987, pp. 57–69.

Sartre, Jean-Paul. *Anti-Semite and Jew*. Trans. George J. Becker. New York: Grove Press, 1962.

———. *Being and Nothingness: A Phenomenological Essay on Ontology*. Trans. Hazel E. Barnes. New York: Washington Square Press, 1966.

———. *The Transcendence of the Ego*. Trans., annotated, and introduced by Forrest Williams and Robert Kirkpatrick. New York: Farrar, Straus, and Giroux, undated. French original published 1936–37.

Schwarzer, Alice. *After "The Second Sex": Conversations with Simone de Beauvoir*. Trans. Marianne Howarth. New York: Pantheon Books, 1984.

Silverman, Hugh J. "Sartre's Words on the Self." In *Jean-Paul Sartre: Contemporary Approaches to His Philosophy*, eds. Hugh J. Silverman and Frederick Elliston. Pittsburgh: Duquesne University Press, 1980, pp. 85–104.

Simons, Margaret A., ed. *Feminist Interpretations of Simone de Beauvoir*. University Park: The Pennsylvania State University Press, 1995.

Spengemann, William C. *The Forms of Autobiography: Episodes in the History of a Literary Genre*. New Haven, CT: Yale University Press, 1980.

Spiegelberg, Herbert. *The Phenomenological Movement*. 2d ed., vol. 1. The Hague: Martinus Nijhoff, 1969.

Stanton, Domna C. "Autogynography: Is the Subject Different?" In *The Female Autograph: Theory and Practice of Autobiography from the Tenth to the Twentieth Century*. Chicago: University of Chicago Press, 1987, pp. 3–20.

Wilder, Thornton. "The Skin of Our Teeth: A Play in Three Acts." In *Three Plays by Thornton Wilder*. New York: Bantam, 1958, pp. 5–137.

Wollstonecraft, Mary. *Vindication of the Rights of Woman*. Ed. and introduced by C. Hagelman, Jr. New York: W. W. Norton, 1967.

Index

About the Author

JO-ANN PILARDI is Professor of Philosophy and Women's Studies at Towson University in Maryland, where she is also Director of Women's Studies. Her main areas of expertise are feminist philosophy, phenomenology and existentialism, postmodernism, and social and political philosophy.